MAKE IT IN PAPER
Creative Three-Dimensional Paper Projects

MAKE IT IN PAPER
Creative Three-Dimensional Paper Projects

MICHAEL GRATER
Illustrated by the Author

DOVER PUBLICATIONS, INC., NEW YORK

Published in Canada by General Publishing Company, Ltd., 30 Lesmill
Road, Don Mills, Toronto, Ontario.
Published in the United Kingdom by Constable and Company, Ltd.

This Dover edition, first published in 1983, is an unabridged and unaltered
republication of the work first published by Mills & Boon Limited, London,
1961, under the title *Make It in Paper: A Simple Introduction to Paper Sculpture for Children, Teachers and Students*.

Manufactured in the United States of America
Dover Publications, Inc., 180 Varick Street, New York, N.Y. 10014

Library of Congress Cataloging in Publication Data

Grater, Michael, 1923–
   Make it in paper.

   Reprint. Originally published: London : Mills & Boon, 1961.
   Summary: Text and illustrations explain techniques used in making three-
dimensional paper toys.
   1. Paper toy making. 2. Paper sculpture. [1. Paper sculpture. 2. Toy
making. 3. Handicraft] I. Title.
TT174.5.P3G7   1983   736′.98   82-18226
ISBN 0-486-24468-7

CONTENTS

FOREWORD

The work compiled in this manuscript has been evolved through several years' practical experiment with children and with teachers.

The results of these experiments have been sifted and simplified so that the introduction of the craft to children requires no previous experience on their part. The work is planned to guide them stage by stage from the most elementary beginning to a point of craftsmanship from which it should be possible for them to branch out on their own.

It has also been planned to be of practical use to those teachers (and student teachers) who are looking for imaginative and new approaches to the work in Art and Craft which they must attempt in schools. The type of work suggested is potentially valuable since it can be undertaken without expensive equipment and is possible where overcrowding or lack of specialist training make the development of interesting schemes of work difficult in practice.

The experiments which I have undertaken with children have been augmented during the past three years by work which I have done with practising teachers. During this time I have been responsible at London University for a course on Creative Work in Schools.

This is an annual thirty-five lecture course and is intended to assist practising teachers in the development of new ideas for creative work with children of all ages. Some of the material which I have included in this manuscript has been taken from work done by teachers on this course, and some of it from work which they have tried in practice in various schools—Infant, Primary and Secondary. The enthusiasm of these teachers for the work, and the successful results which they obtained through its introduction to children, prompted me to plan a course of work and compile it in its present form.

In doing this I have aimed to make it simple and rewarding enough for a child to follow without the aid of a teacher. There are still many children who are anxious to use their leisure time in a constructive way—and still, I hope, many parents who will encourage such an interest.

To assist these children I have made every exercise in the manuscript a creative exercise with an end-product, so that they can enjoy learning the techniques of the craft by watching results emerge as they practise them.

The materials and facilities required for the exercises are simple and inexpensive, and should be available without difficulty in any home or school. *Make It In Paper* could be used by teachers, by children and by students. Its further possible use by adults—club leaders, scouts, party-givers, shop-keepers and window-dressers, or even by parents who merely wish to amuse their own children has also been taken into account in the selection and preparation of the exercises.

M. G.

INTRODUCTION

This is a book for those who like to make things with their hands. It is about the craft of Paper Sculpture and is planned so that a study of the exercises will take an interested student from the first stage—where he knows nothing about the craft—to a point where, having gained certain skills, he will be able to manipulate and mould paper into a variety of interesting and exciting shapes.

Paper sculpture is the craft of raising flat paper into shapes. The tools and materials required are neither complicated nor expensive, and the craft is one that can be practised without any special studio facilities. Unlike the more familiar forms of sculpture it is a craft that can be developed in the home, in almost any room. For an interested student the following materials are all that are necessary:

1.   A supply of paper of fairly good quality. The most satisfactory type is cartridge paper which can be bought in Imperial size sheets (30 in. × 22 in.) from good stationers and artists' suppliers.

2.   Thin cardboard for some of the exercises. This can be of any quality available and can often be salvaged from cartons and packaging materials.

3.   Scissors.

4.   A cutting knife. The type that can be bought with 'throw-away' blades is most suitable, but an ordinary penknife kept reasonably sharp is adequate.

5.   A cutting surface: cardboard, hardboard or, where available, plate-glass.

6.   Gum and transparent sticky tape.

7.   Wire paper-clips and brass paper-fasteners.

8.   Brushes and paints.

9.   A stapling machine as used in offices. This is a useful item but is not essential until considerable skill has been developed in the craft.

There are certain basic techniques in paper sculpture. These are described with suitable exercises in the following pages. They are neither complicated nor difficult, and mastering them requires no previous experience of the craft. The exercises begin from a point where no special artistic ability is needed on the part of a student who is interested enough to attempt them. The suggestions can be studied and tackled by anyone who has no more than an interest in the subject and an ability to find the materials needed.

Given these two things any student can sit down and, through practice, master the techniques which will lead ultimately to his becoming a craftsman in the simple but exciting craft of paper sculpture.

TECHNIQUES

A TECHNIQUE in any craft is the method by which a craftsman uses and controls the materials of his choice in order to make something. For example, a potter 'throwing' or making a pot on a wheel holds his hands in a particular way in order to control the shaping of the clay. If he had no idea of where to place his hands or how to move them as the clay revolved he would be unlikely to produce much of a pot.

If you watch a craftsman potter at work you will see him place his hands without hesitation in a particular position. You will also see that as he moves his hands and the pot takes shape his movements are precise and certain. He knows what he is doing and what he can expect from the clay if he touches it in a certain way. He knows this because he has practised and mastered some of the techniques of his craft.

If you wished to become a potter you would find that the best method of beginning would be to go to the craftsman and ask him to teach you some of the techniques he has already mastered himself. And if he taught you these, how to hold your hands and how to manipulate them on the clay, you would then find it possible, after a period of practice, to make your own pots.

Paper sculpture is a craft in which there are a few basic techniques which you must learn and practise if you wish to attempt any really creative work in paper. These techniques are simple and should take, in each case, only a few minutes to learn. But a little more time must be spent in practising them if they are to be used intelligently and profitably in any subsequent work.

In the following pages the techniques are described separately—with a number of exercises in each of them. The student is recommended to take each technique in turn and to attempt the exercises step by step as illustrated. In this way skill can be acquired gradually, until the point is reached where the craft in its basic form is both mastered and understood.

To make this learning process interesting all the exercises are in themselves opportunities to make something in paper. Each time you complete an exercise you will have a model in front of you. You will have made it yourself, and every piece of work finished will be evidence of a little more skill gained in the craft. It is this skill which will enable you, once you have mastered all the techniques, to create almost anything you wish from a few pieces of paper. You will be a craftsman and at that point you will be able to put this book away and use your own imagination in the development of further work.

But you should begin first with the exercises, practising and understanding the possibilities of each technique and really mastering it before going on to attempt the next.

THE SCORE

To the sculptor one of the qualities necessary in his work is that it should have what is called FORM. Pick up an object, a vase or an ornament or a toy, and hold it in your two hands. You will understand what is meant by saying that an object has form if you continue to hold it and at the same time close your eyes. Even though you can no longer see the object you can feel the form. It is there all the time, all round the object. And it is the form that you can feel which allows you to identify and recognise the shape which you are holding.

A sheet of paper is flat and has no form. But if you fold the paper down the centre and make it stand on end—like a Christmas card on a mantelpiece—you will find that it now has a simple form and can be seen or touched from any angle—front, sides or back.

This is, in simple terms, what the paper sculptor is trying to achieve. He is trying to convert the flat shape into something which has form.

But folding the paper by hand is not precise or clean enough. In paper sculpture a technique known as SCORING is used to achieve the cleanest possible fold.

In this technique, using the point of a knife, a cut is made into the surface of the paper along the exact line of the fold. This cut must only break the surface and must at no point penetrate the whole thickness of the paper. For this reason it is sometimes called the HALF-CUT.

In paper sculpture the half-cut or score enables a clean fold to be made and is used for two purposes:

1. The fold gives added strength to the paper—and support in modelling. You can demonstrate this for yourself by taking an ordinary sheet of notepaper. You will find it difficult to make this sheet stand on its edge without support of some kind. But if you fold the paper along the line of its centre it will stand easily, like the Christmas card already mentioned. The fold has given the paper its own support.

2. Used in various ways the fold gives interest by allowing for development of a variety of forms. You will see this best demonstrated for yourself as you attempt the exercises in the use of the score.

To begin with you should practise scoring on any scraps of paper. The knife blade is best used rather like the point of a pencil, almost as though it is being used to draw the actual line of the fold. For straight scoring a ruler may be used as a guide. But later exercises will require free-hand scoring on curved folds, and it is advisable not to become too dependent on a ruler in the early stages.

It is usual in paper sculpture to fold the paper away from the actual cut of the score—so that the paper can open very slightly along the line of the cut. If you find after scoring that the paper has been cut through at any point on the fold you are applying too much pressure as you draw the blade over the surface. A little practice should show you the exact amount of pressure needed to make a neat and effective score. You will quickly learn that a sharp knife will go right through one thickness of cartridge paper under very little pressure. But you can only be sure of the exact pressure required by practising with the knife and paper.

Fig. 1. SCORING—When making a score the knife must only break the surface of the paper; it must not cut right through. In order to avoid unnecessary pressure it is useful to practise holding the knife like a pen when scoring.

Exercises in the use of the Straight Score

When you are able to make a piece of paper stand by scoring and folding you can begin some simple paper sculpture. For your first real exercise you can make some simple standing figures. These can be attempted in cartridge paper or in thin cardboard and, like all paper sculpture, they will be most effective if kept simple and not too complicated.

You know by now that a rectangle of paper scored and folded at the line of its centre will stand without any additional support. You can now draw a simple outline on one side of the folded paper and can cut round the outline to make a shape (see overleaf).

This shape should be kept simple, since if you cut away too much of the original paper, you will defeat the object of strengthening the paper by scoring—and your model will be too weak to stand without support. It should be possible with reasonably sharp scissors to cut both sides of the model in one operation.

Fig. 2. A rectangle of paper scored down its centre (dotted line in diagram) will stand upright, and can be cut and decorated to make a simple shape.

After cutting, the model can be decorated or coloured in any way you like, and can be given further suggestions of form as in an ordinary drawing—eyes, nose, etc. If you use a good quality paper it should be possible to cut the model ten to twelve inches in height, but models taller than this will probably need to be made in cardboard.

When you have made and decorated one figure you can amuse yourself by making

Fig. 3. The standing shapes can be varied in appearance by cutting from rectangles of different sizes, and by the use of imaginative decoration.

a whole family of different shapes and sizes. This will give you practice in scoring and in cutting, and will furthermore allow you to exercise your own imagination. This is something you must try to do as you attempt the exercises in this book.

In this instance, if you find it difficult to make much variety in your imaginary figures, you should think of people you know and use these for models. You must not expect to get much of a likeness. But remembering individual people—whether they are tall and thin or short and fat, the kind of clothes they wear, and so on—will give you a point from which to start the exercises.

In this exercise you must not make the legs of the figures too thin or the feet too small. Otherwise the models will not stand. But you need not worry about this. Your models will be recognisable as figures even though you make the legs thick and the feet large. This can, in fact, be part of the pleasure of the exercise. In paper sculpture you can exaggerate where you want to or where it is necessary. It is a light-hearted craft which should never attempt to be too serious or too realistic. It should be fun to please yourself what you do with a shape, and every exercise you attempt should amuse you a little. For this reason any decoration you add should be gay and—if you have the materials— colourful and with plenty of pattern. It is never a waste of time to make something bright and cheerful. It will give pleasure to someone, even if it is only to yourself. And you will learn best if your exercises in technique are amusing and light-hearted. Most of us know from experience that learning tedious things is a very difficult business and one that requires a lot of application and effort.

Paper sculpture is not tedious. And working through the exercises will not be a dull business unless you make it unnecessarily so.

When you have made a family of standing figures you can introduce a little more variety into your work by cutting into the score as well as at the edge of your shape.

Fig. 4. A shape drawn on one side of the rectangle can be cut with the paper folded double. Additional visual interest can be given to the shape by cutting into the score.

In the head of the clown (Fig. 4) you can cut into the score where you have drawn the nose and the mouth.

The lines on the diagram show how these cuts can be made. If you make them the same as the diagram you will find that, after cutting, part of the mouth will drop away but that the nose will remain as part of the shape. After decorating the model you will find it possible to give added interest by pulling the nose slightly forward away from the shape.

You can try further exercises like this in a variety of different shapes and sizes. If you sit in front of a mirror and make faces at yourself you will see that a mouth may be drawn in a variety of shapes. And if you paint and decorate the clowns in an extraordinary way you will be doing no more to your models than real clowns do to their own faces before they go into the ring at a circus.

When you have finished a number of clowns you can use them to decorate your room. They can be very attractive and are particularly useful if you are having a party.

As a further exercise you can, after making the heads of the clowns, attempt the rest of the circus. It is all good practice in mastering and using the technique. This is the way a craft works. It begins with materials and technique and afterwards an idea is developed in which both these things are put together in order to create or make something.

Fig. 5. An interesting variety of standing shapes can be developed on a single idea. This type of project is valuable as an exercise in developing an imaginative approach to the possibilities of the techniques being practised.

You can now make your clown's head into a standing clown—as you made the standing figures when you started to learn the technique of scoring. Still thinking of the circus, you can take another figure: the strong man, making him suitably squat and bulky and painting on him the right sort of costume. In this case you must cut into the score as well as the sides in order to show his arms holding up the weights. From the strong man you can go on to the acrobats, and this time you can make two figures—one supporting the other; but you must cut them both together from one piece of paper. When you go on to the animals there are many shapes you can attempt, so long as you remember that you have as yet only one simple technique to use. For this reason your shapes must still be very simple, like the lion (Fig. 5) with the score and part-fold down the centre of the shape. But you can have many different animals sitting on different shapes, and the shapes can be highly decorated as they are in the circus. If you look closely at the lion in the illustration you will notice that his tail is—as it should be—only on one side, although the shape was originally cut double. You can, of course, snip bits off here and there if you need to in the model. In this case the tail on one side has been cut away.

To develop the circus further you can try other shapes of your own: the Ring-Master, or some performing seals with balls balanced on their snouts, or a nicely striped tiger. There are many others you can attempt if you think all round the idea of the circus.

If you prefer you can use the same technique on another idea. You can try a military band in brightly coloured uniforms, or a scene from a play, or a fancy dress parade, or characters in historical costume. You can make a forest of different shaped trees—but in these the trunks must not be cut too thin. There are many ideas you can discover for yourself as you practise and learn to use the technique.

If you enjoy painting patterns you can choose ideas which give you plenty of opportunity for pattern work. For example an aviary of imaginary birds will offer a great deal of scope for exciting colour and pattern.

Models like these are best made in paper and not cardboard, since they should be cut with the paper folded on the score—so that the two sides of the model are identical. This makes for a pleasing finish—when both sides of the model have the same pattern of cuts—and at this stage in your work you should already be aiming for a pleasing effect in the finished model.

For this reason also you should paint your models with as much care as possible. Untidy work is never very satisfying, either to the person who does it—or to others who might see the work in its finished state. It helps to keep your pattern tidy if you are aware of the actual shape of the model as you do your painting. You should if possible try to make some of the pattern flow with the shape you have cut so that it helps to emphasise and not break the shape. A pattern which fits a shape is less likely to jar in the finished effect than one which is painted on without any thought to the shape of the background.

In this type of exercise—and in later ones where you will be asked to make animal shapes—it is helpful in the finished effect if you make the eyes as clear as possible—even to the point of exaggeration. A large eye with a simple white eyeball and a dark pupil is always more effective and rewarding than any amount of fussy and unnecessary detail in the painting.

When you have really mastered the first part of the technique of scoring—and if you have completed the exercises you will have done this—you will have finished a number of models. You need not throw them away when you go on to the next part of the technique. If they are not too large you can keep them and use them as invitation or greetings cards. You can write an appropriate message on the side that you did not decorate—and you can be sure that when your friends receive them they will be delighted and intrigued.

Fig. 6. Further visual effect can be given to standing shapes by making interesting cuts into the edges of the form. When decorating these, and subsequent exercises, attention should be paid to the nature of the pattern used. It should be designed to fit and flow with the shape so that the finished effect is pleasing. This effect will be certain if the decoration is made to grow from the shape so that it seems to be an essential part of the whole.

In fact, now that you have mastered this simple technique you need never buy another Christmas card. You should be enough of a craftsman by now to make very original ones of your own. A Father Christmas, an angel, a choir-boy, a fat postman, a turkey, a plum pudding with a face appearing over its top—any of these and many others are possible if you use this simple technique of scoring and cutting on the fold.

CURVING THE SCORE

The SCORE as used in paper sculpture need not be straight.

If you cut two identical leaf shapes you can score one of them with a straight line down its centre. In this instance you do not make the score in order to stand the leaf as you did with the figures in the previous exercises. You make the score so that you can

Fig. 7. A straight score may be used to give form to a flat shape, but it is possible to raise a more interesting form by curving the score. This must be done by drawing free-hand with the knife, and will require a little practice before the technique is mastered.

part-fold the leaf to show two surfaces on one shape. After scoring and folding, the surfaces meet at an angle. These surfaces are called PLANES; and if you hold the leaf away from you, you will see that one of the planes is slightly darker than the other. If you try this in a room where the light comes from a window you will see that the plane nearer the window is lighter than the other. This is an example of a contrast in tone which makes the leaf more interesting visually than the shape was before scoring.

If you now take the same shape and make your score with a free-hand curve—like the second shape in the illustration—you will find it possible to bend the leaf along the line of the score into an even more interesting shape. This bending is a form of modelling and you must learn to do it rather delicately with your fingers, taking care not to force or buckle the paper. The fold must be made only along the line of the score, and if this is done carefully you will see that, unlike the first shape, it is not possible with this type of score to fold the leaf double. It is possible, however, to fold it sufficiently off the flat to make an interesting contrast of planes in the shape.

For the beginner it will probably be necessary to try this several times before the planes can be made to contrast neatly. But when this can be done successfully subsequent exercises can become slightly more creative and interesting.

Exercises in Curving the Score

For your first real exercise in the use of a curved score you can take a strip of paper twelve to eighteen inches long and three or four inches wide. A long curving score can then be made down the centre of the strip. If you are not too confident of your ability to control your knife at this stage you can draw the line of the score very lightly with a pencil before cutting.

When you have made the score draw an outline and cut the strip into an eel-like shape (see opposite page).

After cutting you can decorate the model before part-folding along the line of the score. If the score is neat the model will curve just enough to give a suggestion of wriggling. And this curve, although cut in the original shape, is greatly assisted when the planes are contrasted along the line of the score.

If the model is successful it can be fixed to a wall or a window with transparent sticky tape, or it can be fixed to a curtain with ordinary dressmaker's pins. These models you make in paper should not present any difficulty when you want to fix them somewhere. They have so little weight that they are easily secured with pins or with sticky tape.

As you attempt this and subsequent exercises with the curved score you must understand that this technique is primarily intended to allow modelling of the paper. But like the straight score it does give slightly added strength to the paper. Therefore if you apply an uneven pressure when you are scoring and cut right through the surface at any point, you make a weakness in the model and defeat part of the object of the technique. If this is the case further practice is necessary in order to master the technique.

The exercise illustrated (Fig. 9) shows how to model a crab-like shape using the same technique as in the previous exercise. In the diagram the dotted lines indicate the points at which the shape must be scored and part-folded. When cutting the outline shape you

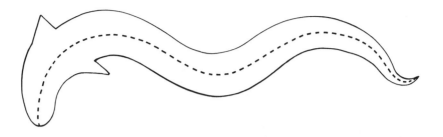

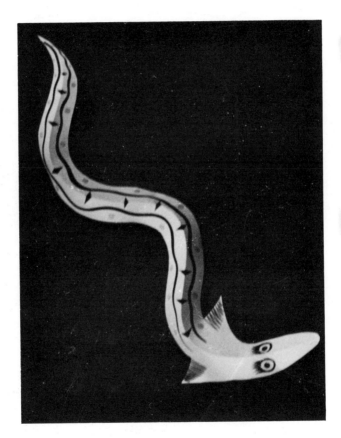

Fig. 8. Practice in the curved score can be gained from the development of interesting shapes, since the technique allows for the introduction into paper of a flowing quality.

should notice that the cut making the top of each claw is made into the body shape and meets the score on both sides.

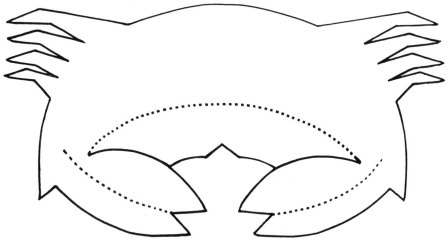

Fig. 9. Techniques can be practised creatively to produce interesting shapes. The dotted lines on the diagram indicate the curved scores which will enable you to raise this crab-like form from flat paper. Decoration can be applied before or after scoring.

To follow this and other diagrams in the book requires no more than a little careful concentration. They need be studied only until they make sense and are understood, and afterwards need not be copied with absolute accuracy. They are not rules, but are intended rather as a series of guides to help you practise the techniques you are learning.

It is because they illustrate possible methods of using the techniques that you must know what you are doing when you cut the shapes indicated in the diagrams. For your purpose understanding them is in fact better than copying them accurately—although this is of course permissible when you attempt the exercises.

In the crab-like shape you should understand that the lower scores will enable you to curve the claws upwards from the original flat shape; and that the upper score when folded will enable you to raise the body and give it—by contrasted planes—some suggestion of form.

On this model you can again add any decoration you wish. But once more you should remember to make the eyes as large and as bold as possible.

If you looked really closely at the diagram before drawing and cutting this exercise you might have noticed that both sides of the model are the same. This might have prompted you to fold the paper at the centre in order to cut both the sides at once. Although there is no rule about this and it might appear a sensible thing to do, it is in this instance undesirable—since a vertical fold on the model will tend to spoil the curve made by the score on the body.

If you find it difficult to make the two sides similar without folding and cutting the shape double you can assist yourself by making two models. The first one, folded and cut in one operation, can be opened out and placed flat on an unfolded piece of paper. When it is flat you can draw round it and use it as a guide or TEMPLATE, but while you are drawing round it you must hold it very still if you want to get an accurate reproduction of the shape on your second piece of paper.

You will find this method of making a template before cutting the actual model useful in later exercises. And since the templates are intended only to serve as preliminary guides to the models they can be made in any scraps of unwanted paper. If it is not too creased wrapping paper is quite suitable—or the covers of old magazines may be used. It is certainly not necessary to use your best quality paper in the preparation of templates in this or any subsequent exercise.

If you attempt the following exercise you will find that a curved score can be made large enough to give considerable form to a flat piece of paper.

To make the frog in this exercise the score must be a little more than a half-circle as shown in the dotted line in Fig. 10 on page 24. If you are unsure of your ability to make this score with a free-hand cut, a simple template can be used as a guide. A template can also be used to draw the actual shape for the frog, but you must notice that on this shape two cuts are made into the body of the paper. It is these two cuts that make the legs of the frog when the form of the body is raised on the large score.

To raise the body it must first be part-folded at the score. It will then be possible to pull the two sides of the model together to meet in the middle, where they can be fixed with a paper fastener. The points to be pulled together are on the main body of the frog—not on the legs, which should be allowed to lie loosely at the sides of the body.

The act of pulling and fixing the sides of the body together will raise the model considerably from the flat; and the area inside the curve of the score will form a funnel-like opening which can suggest the mouth of the frog.

Fig. 10. The curved score can be used
to give considerable form to a flat
piece of paper. The form in this
frog-like shape can be raised by
scoring a large curve, enabling the
sides of the model to be drawn
together and fixed at the centre.
Further form can be introduced
into the model by scoring along
the centre of the legs.

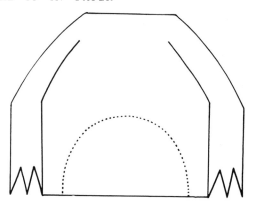

This is a rather exaggerated model. But if you make it in coloured paper and add large, frog-like eyes it should be recognisable—although it might help to know that the top part of the diagram is the back end of the frog. In the model as shown in the diagram there are no front legs. These have been omitted deliberately since they would be an unnecessary complication at this stage in the exercises. As you learn the techniques of paper sculpture you will begin to realise that this is a craft in which it is always desirable to simplify as much as possible. This can usually be taken to the point of leaving out things which are apparently quite important to a model—as in this case: the front legs of the frog. They are not vital and would tend to make the model complicated both in construction and in its final appearance.

It is sometimes helpful when cutting a score on a pointed projection of paper to cut the bottom of the paper on one side from the outer edge of the shape to the score. This cut, used in the right way will allow greater flexibility when part of a model has to be folded on a curved score.

This is illustrated in Fig. 11, which is a suggested way for you to cut a windmill. The example is still an exercise in the use of the curved score—there are, in fact, four places which require this type of score. But if you look closely at the diagram you will notice that you must cut into the paper as far as the score at the base of each of the scored shapes. The illustration shows how each of these shapes can then be part-folded on the score to make two planes.

Fig. 11. As a further exercise in scoring, the same shape can be cut four times in one piece of paper. The curved portions can be part-folded and will act as sails so that the shape will revolve on a pin like a toy windmill. In this exercise cuts made from the bottom edges of the tail-shapes to the scores assist the process of raising form in the shapes.

If you follow the diagram you will find it possible to make a shape that suggests a group of four cats sitting in a circle—and each of the cats has a curved form raised in its tail. This is again merely an exercise for you to practise the technique of curved scoring. But if you decorate the model and put a pin through it at the centre it can be made to behave like the toy windmills which are sold for very young children. This is because the four tails with their curved forms can act as sails.

To make the windmill turn effectively in the wind you should put a small disc of paper or card at the front between the model and the head of the pin. You should also have a separating piece behind the model—a section cut from an ordinary drinking straw will do—so that as it revolves the windmill will not touch the surface into which it is pinned.

For this model you will almost certainly need to cut a template, and if you look closely at the diagram you can see how this can be done with the aid of a compass. The model can be cut from a circle divided into four equal parts. The lines at the bottom of the tails can be marked on an inner circle.

You can therefore begin your template by drawing a circle and using a ruler to divide it into four equal parts. Using the same centre point you can then draw an inner circle, and from this stage it should not be difficult to draw in the rest of the diagram.

When you consider this exercise you might ask why a paper sculptor should bother to cut and make a toy windmill. There is no real reason other than that of cutting an interesting shape which provides further opportunity to practise the technique of curved scoring.

The forms raised by the scores can be made to behave in an amusing way if you make the example suggested, which is a way of adding interest to the practical exercise in order to help you enjoy the craft as you learn it.

As a final exercise in the technique of scoring you can take a shape which will allow for the development of variations of your own, according to the way you cut the shape and make the scores.

The cow-like head shown in Fig. 12 incorporates a number of scores and you can, if you wish, make your first one exactly like that shown in the diagram.

In this shape you should pay particular attention to the score at the bottom of the diagram. When this score is part-folded it will be possible to bend the two outer points inwards to meet at the back. Care must be taken not to buckle the paper, which should be handled gently so that the curves made by the scores raise two definite shapes. These two shapes, like circles disappearing behind the mask, will suggest rather large nostrils—an example of simple exaggeration in the craft. And to hold them in place you must use gum or sticky tape to fix the points where they meet at the back.

The top score will allow you to part-fold and curve the horn-shapes slightly forward. You will find it helps in this part of the model to make a cut on the centre line from the top edge down to this score.

You can also score and give form to the ears, although these are not essential and may be left out if you find the model too complicated.

The score down the centre of the mask will strengthen the paper enough to allow you to model this example without its becoming too floppy or unwieldy. With good

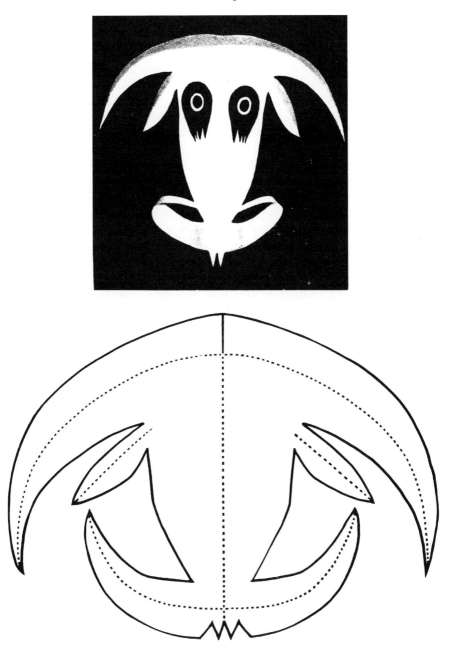

Fig. 12. To make the cow's head it is necessary to incorporate a number of scores into one model so that form of various types is given to different parts of the original shape. The basic technique can be used on shapes of different proportions so that a variety of effects may be achieved.

quality paper it should be possible to make the model from twelve to eighteen inches high. This score will also allow you to cut the model double so that both sides are exactly the same.

If you can complete a mask like this you have mastered your first technique and you are ready to go on to the next exercises. But before doing this you could profitably spend a little time experimenting with the shape and introducing variations of your own. Instead of following the diagram exactly you can, for example, use it as a guide to make a longer and thinner mask. Or you can make one in which the horns curve up instead of down.

You must remember that as you progress in learning the techniques you should be prepared to make simple experiments in their use on models you can adapt or devise for yourself.

There are still other techniques for you to learn, as there are many exercises to give you practice in the craft. But as soon as you have an idea of your own you must be ready to try it out. This is as important a part of your development as a craftsman as is the business of attempting the set exercises. The two things will at some point begin to go together. But this need not happen yet. There is still plenty of time, and if you find you are not yet ready for experiments of your own, there is no reason to worry. This point will come at some stage as you progress. And in the meantime you must go on with the exercises.

In any case you are now ready to learn and practise a further technique. But as you begin this you should not forget the work you have already done on the various uses of the technique of SCORING.

THE CUT TO CENTRE

In previous exercises it was demonstrated that Form can be raised in flat paper through the technique of Scoring and part-folding. A further method of raising form from the flat is by means of the technique known as the 'Cut to Centre'.

To demonstrate this you should draw a circle on a flat piece of paper and cut it out. A compass may be used to make the drawing a perfect circle, which should have a radius of from three to six inches.

If you place the circle you have cut on a table you will see that it is a flat disc; it has shape but it has no form. To give the disc form you can make one cut from any point on its edge to the centre; and for this cut you can use either a knife or a pair of scissors.

If you now hold the two sides of the cut—one in each hand—and pull them together to overlap you will find that the flat disc becomes a cone; and will remain a cone if you fasten the paper at the point of overlap. The flat disc of paper has been given form.

The paper sculptor secures the overlap by fastening in one of three ways:
 i. By punching the paper together with a staple from an office-type stapling machine.
 ii. By inserting a small brass paper-fastener and opening the points on the inside of the cone.
 iii. By gumming with any type of paper gum. In this method he will use a paper clip to hold the overlap in place until the gum has dried.

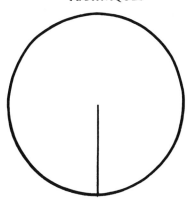

Fig. 13. CUT TO CENTRE—Flat paper can be given form by cutting from the edge to the centre and overlapping the side of the cut.

Fig. 14. Form raised by cutting to the centre and overlapping can be secured by:
   (i) Stapling.
  (ii) Inserting a brass paper-fastener.
 (iii) Gumming—in this method the sides of the overlap must be held together with a paper clip until the gum has dried.

This method of cutting to the centre and overlapping to give form is not limited to circular shapes. It can be used effectively with almost any shape, but it is useful in the first stages to learn and understand the technique by practising on the circle. This is a shape which behaves well in this technique; and it should be practised until it becomes a simple matter to produce and fix cones which are neat and which show no sign of distortion or buckling.

Exercises in the Cut to Centre

As you practise making cones you should experiment to see how small or how large they can be made effectively. You should also try experiments in raising the height of the form in a cone by increasing the overlap—or lowering it by decreasing.

These are merely exercises in technique but they can be made interesting if a little time is spent decorating some of the finished cones. If they are painted on both sides and strung together, one above the other with a suitable space between them, they can be used as simple but effective hanging decorations.

If you prefer you can use your imagination to make them into shapes that say something—like the clown or the tiger.

Fig. 15. Practice in raising form by cutting to the centre can be made interesting if the cones are treated imaginatively after fixing.

You will notice that the clown suggested in the illustration has a second cone which might be fixed above him with a stick or a drinking straw. This cone can be decorated by snipping a cut pattern round the edge.

By now you should be able to attempt your own improvements and additions to the models you make. You can notice, for example, how the top of the tiger cone might be cut to suggest a hairy back. In the same way part of the base can be cut away to suggest the position of the legs. Anything like this is permissible so long as it adds interest to the model and does not make it unnecessarily untidy.

You will find that these personal touches will come gradually as you develop skill and confidence in the craft. When an idea occurs to you it should be tried in practice. But you must remember that some experiments will fail. It is from these failures that you will learn what you cannot do—as you learn what you can do by trying the exercises.

The guiding factor in all your work must be that it is permissible to attempt anything with your models, providing that any treatment you apply adds to the visual interest of the end product. But while attempting any improvements or variations of your own as you experiment you should aim always for a crisp and clean finish in all your work. If you do this you will not only master the techniques of the craft but will also develop a standard of appreciation and criticism. These two things are both essential factors in the further development of confidence and ability in the craft, and will bolster and support the ability you are already gaining in the use of techniques.

After learning to raise a flat disc to a cone you can apply the same technique to other shapes in paper.

If you take, for example, a square and cut it on the diagonal from one corner to the centre you will find, on overlapping the cut edges, that the flat shape may be given form in the shape of a shield.

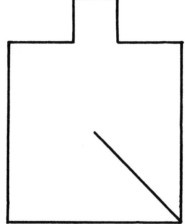

Fig. 16. The cut to centre can be used on a variety of flat shapes. When the cut is made on the diagonal from a corner to the centre of a square the form raised will take that of a shield.

As a further exercise in the use of this technique you can try this with squares of different sizes. And these can be made interesting if they are painted as wall decorations. When painting them it is necessary to note that any decoration drawn on the square before overlapping will look odd when the form is raised to become a shield. If you try this for yourself it should not be difficult to find a method of overcoming this problem.

In the diagram (Fig. 16) you will notice that an extra piece of paper has been left at the top of the square. You will find it useful to incorporate such an extra piece when cutting your squares if you want to fix the finished shields to a background.

By bending the extra portion down behind the shield it can be pinned to the background as an invisible fixture—since the shield itself will hide the pin.

This method of hiding fixtures helps to make the end product neat and is, in fact, one of the techniques of paper sculpture. If you adopt the technique of adding an extra flap in this instance you should remember it for future use—since you will find it introduced and illustrated in more detail in later exercises.

If you understand how form can be raised by cutting to the centre of a flat shape you can, in your next exercise, apply the technique to a simple example of real paper sculpture.

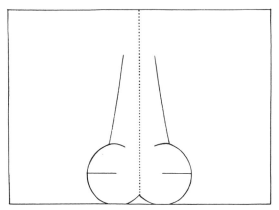

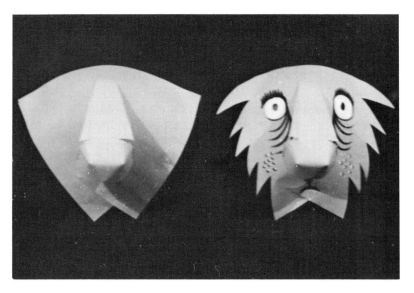

Fig. 17. In this exercise on cutting to the centre, form can be raised in two ways from the rectangle. Further cutting and decoration can make this form into a mask.

The diagram (Fig. 17) shows a rectangle of paper with a vertical score at the centre indicated by the dotted line. In this exercise the model must be treated in an identical way on both sides and, if you use the score, you can do this by folding your paper double. In this way any cuts you make will be the same on both sides of the score.

If you look closely at the diagram you will notice that the circles touching the bottom line are incomplete. You will also notice that if they were complete they would overlap the line of the score.

These circles, which can be drawn with a compass, are incomplete because the lines indicated are actually the lines you must cut. If the circles were complete and you were to cut right round them they would drop out of the rectangle and be of no use in the model. You must be sure, therefore, to leave the unmarked parts uncut so that the circles remain as part of the model.

The horizontal lines on the circles indicate the points at which they must be cut to the centre. A cut must also be made from the top of each circle towards the upper edge of the rectangle at a slight angle as indicated in the diagram.

These cuts are not as complicated as they may appear, and can be done quite easily by following with a little care the black lines indicated on the diagram.

When you have completed the cuts you can raise both the circles to cones as you did in the first exercise in this technique.

Now place the paper in front of you and overlap the bottom pieces of the rectangle underneath the section on which you have made the cones.

Your original rectangle will now have two lots of form: one made by the centre strip with the two cones at its end, and the other made by overlapping the two sides of the rectangle.

This will give you a basic shape for a mask, the two cones and the strip above them suggesting nostrils at the end of a nose. As a mask this is really more suitable for an animal than for a human shape. And you can see in the illustration how a few cuts at the edges of the shape and a little painted decoration can make the suggestion of a lion's head from the shape shown in the original diagram.

When you have completed this exercise you should understand that by using certain techniques you have actually completed a piece of work in paper sculpture. You have taken a flat piece of paper and you have given it form which suggests a real shape. This is, in fact, sculpture in paper.

Fig. 18, overleaf, illustrates a further exercise in which you can combine all the techniques you have so far practised. The beetle shape can be cut with the paper scored and folded double so that the sides are identical. The black line on the circle indicates where it must be cut to the centre (on both sides of the model), and the dotted line where you must make a curved score on the claw shapes. This score must be made at both sides with the paper opened out flat after cutting.

The circles cut to the centre can be overlapped and raised to give form to the eyes, which can be painted with dark pupils at their centres. The claws can be part-folded along the lines of the scores.

When you have applied these techniques your model should have form in three places: in the eyes, in the claws and along the back at the first centre score. You can now decorate the rest of the shape as you wish. This is made easier if you cut the beetle from coloured paper in the first place.

As a further development of the exercise you can try cutting the shape to include legs. These can be developed even further by scoring and part-folding, although they are not essential to the model. You can include them if you wish. You can also vary the exercise by cutting the beetles in shapes which are different from the one illustrated.

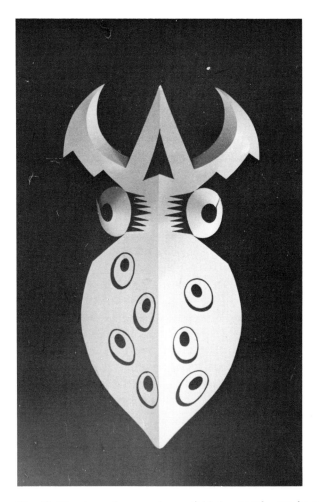

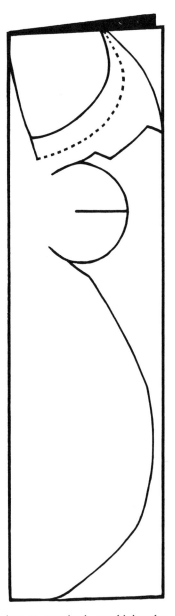

Fig. 18. The shape shown, cut on a folded rectangle, can be used as an exercise in combining the
techniques of SCORING and CUTTING TO CENTRE. The use of both techniques is a means of
giving form to different parts of the shape, in the eyes and in the claws. Further form can be
retained in the shape from the original score at the centre.

A reference book with suitable illustrations might give you ideas for further variations,
although the exercise should still be planned to retain the combined use of the techniques
as shown in the example illustrated.

A number of these beetle shapes, if they are attractively decorated, can be pinned to curtains or cushions as unusual and amusing decorations for a party. They need not be large. It should be possible to cut one or two of them from a sheet of paper the size of this page.

THE RETURN

If you attempted the exercises in the technique of cutting to the centre you will remember that you were recommended to include a small flap of paper at the top of the square (Fig. 16) in order to provide an invisible fixture for the model.

The inclusion of this extra piece of paper is an example of the technique known as the RETURN, which is used where possible by paper sculptors to keep their models neat. A work of paper sculpture may be ruined if every point at which it has been necessary to make a join or fixture can be seen in the finished model. In most cases the correct use of a RETURN can successfully disguise any join in the paper.

It is obviously not difficult to include an extra flap of paper when cutting a shape. The difficulty is to anticipate exactly where a return should be incorporated into the flat shape. For this reason it is again necessary to understand the technique. You can learn it in a few minutes. But in order to apply its use successfully in later modelling of your own, you are recommended to study the placing of the returns and their uses stage by stage in the exercises given.

Fig. 19a

Exercises in the Return

In the first exercise the diagrams (Fig. 19) show four shapes which can be cut and joined to make a simple cat-like mask. It should be noted that although many of the exercises shown so far have involved the use of only one shape, it is sometimes necessary in more advanced work to build the model by combining a number of pieces into one.

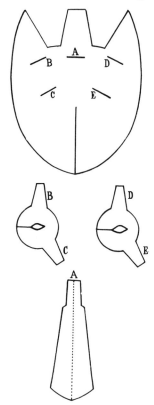

Fig. 19b

Fig. 19b. Component parts of a model can be fitted together by cutting RETURNS on the shapes and inserting them through corresponding slots in the shapes into which they are to be fitted. In the exercise illustrated, returns are marked to correspond with their appropriate slots.

Of the four shapes shown in the diagram the largest one at the top is the base on which the others must be built to make the mask. The vertical cut from the bottom into this shape is the one which will enable you to give it form by overlapping. The return at the top of the shape will allow you to make an invisible fixture after completing the model.

The circles under the main shape are the eyes—cut to the centre so that they can be made up into cones. In this case an extra cut can be made at the centre of each eye as shown in order to suggest the pupil. This is a development on previous methods which illustrates the desirability of doing as much of the modelling as possible in the paper without the use of additional materials. You will find on raising the cones that the portion cut away at the centre will leave a hole exactly where it would have been necessary to paint in the pupil.

The eye shapes are each shown with two returns. The positioning of the top return will be obvious. But you must notice that the lower one is off-centre. It is included in the original flat shape slightly to one side so that it will be in the centre and opposite the top one when the shape is raised to a cone by overlapping.

The bottom shape in the diagram illustrates the method of cutting a simple nose, scored at the centre to give form, and with a return included at the top.

If you cut these shapes with the returns as shown it is a simple matter to fix them together by cutting slots at appropriate points in the basic shape. The returns can be inserted into these slots to hold the parts together and can be folded out of sight at the back.

It is important to position these slots carefully before cutting, as it is important to position the returns on the component parts. In the case of the eyes the cones should be raised and gummed. When they are ready for attaching to the main shape the returns should be folded outwards from the base of each cone. The cone should then be placed on the background shape, and when it is in the correct position the points at which the returns join the eyes should be pricked with a pin into the background. If the cones are then removed the pin holes will show the exact points at which the slots must be cut.

The same method can be used in positioning the nose. After holding it in place against the background and pricking with a pin you can cut the slots for the return with the point of a knife, but care must be taken to make the cut exactly between the pin holes.

After the returns have been inserted through the slots they can be bent over at the back and will hold the added pieces in shape although they will not be visible. If the model is to be kept the returns can be gummed at the back as a permanent fixture.

For a background colour almost anything will be effective. Paper sculpture is a decorative craft, and models do not have to conform in colour to their counterparts in real life.

In this exercise the cat could, for example, be cut with white eyes against a bright red background. Normal cats, of course, do not have bright red faces. But the artist or craftsman who makes a cat does not make a normal one, and he is always at liberty to please himself in his choice of colour.

You can see this yourself in the ornaments in your home. A china cat might have pink spots or green stripes. This is part of the pleasure of decorative things. They are not real. And because they are decorations, we can accept oddities in colours and patterning.

The same applies in paper sculpture. A decorative effect and colour somewhat removed from real life will add to the attraction and appeal of models made in the craft. There are no rules. The only limit on colours you may choose for your exercises will lie in the choice of coloured papers at your disposal.

As further exercises in the use of the return you can make a variety of masks by evolving basic shapes and additions of your own, although you should make the exercises valuable by incorporating the techniques you have learned so far.

Fig. 20, next page shows a number of basic shapes suitable for making up a human mask, with the returns marked to correspond with the slots into which they should be fitted.

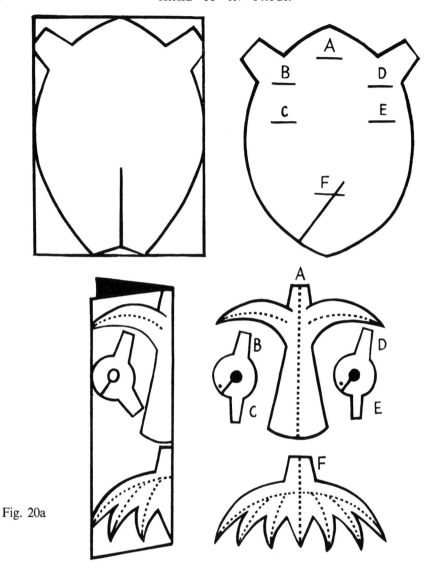

Fig. 20a

Fig. 20. For exercises it saves waste to cut as many shapes as possible from one piece of paper. But where contrast is important in the final version it may be necessary to cut shapes separately.

You will notice that the eyes, nose and moustache shapes can be cut from one rectangle of paper scored and folded at the centre. For practice in the technique this is a satisfactory method since it avoids any unnecessary waste of paper. But for later, more effective results you should investigate the possibility of varying your colour as you design and cut your shapes. In the example shown it would obviously be more effective to cut the nose the same colour as the background, the eyes white and the moustache black.

Fig. 20b

This mask is a development on the previous exercise in that it can have scored eyebrows above the eyes. This gives added interest to the model, besides being an exercise in a technique you have already learned. The moustache can also be improved by scoring and raising form on each of its points.

In the diagram a return is left on each side of the basic shape. These will enable you to put a string round the back of the mask so that you can wear it if you wish. You can do this after completing the exercise or, if you prefer, you can make a number of different masks which can be used as decorations. In this case it would only be necessary to leave one return at the top of the basic shape.

If you include both returns so that you can wear the mask you must consider the need to be able to see through it. There is only one way to solve this problem, and it is one you can quite easily work out for yourself.

You may wonder, if you have attempted most of the previous exercises, why none of them has been shown incorporating a shape suitable for a mouth.

This omission is a deliberate example of the way the paper sculptor tries to work. It again illustrates the technique of simplification; but again there is no rule. It is merely a matter of controlling the number of separate pieces which go into a model and eliminating anything which is unnecessary.

If you look, for example, at the mask you made (Fig. 20) you can see that it is without doubt a simplified version of a type of face. The moustache shape is simple to cut and fix. It is immediately understood, and the fact that it is positioned under the nose automatically suggests the presence of a mouth. The addition of a further shape for a mouth would only complicate the model, and nothing would be gained from it in the finished effect.

If we can accept this model as a mask it is because we are able to take for granted those parts which have been left out. We understand what we see, and this stimulates us enough to imagine the rest.

In paper sculpture as much as possible should be left to the imagination. It is impossible to achieve accuracy in every detail; and you should aim, therefore, at a simple statement of the main characteristics of the shape to be modelled—exaggerating, where possible, the more important of these characteristics. You can see this in the mask with the large moustache; where a simple shape—cut and folded in an interesting way and fixed in the right place—establishes a type.

In aiming for this type of simplification you must understand that any detail left out is omitted only because it is unnecessary and not because it is too difficult to make. If you feel that a mouth is essential in your mask you must experiment with the techniques you know until you have developed a satisfactory shape for this purpose. You must remember at the same time to include a return when you cut the shape so that it can be fixed neatly under the moustache.

CURLING

The next technique you must learn is that used in the treatment of flat paper in order to give it what appears to be a natural curl.

You can try this first of all with a strip of paper about an inch wide and eight or nine inches long. If you hold an end of the strip in one hand and draw the blade of a knife along the under surface of the paper—making the movement from the point where it is held towards the free end—the paper will, when released, spring back and curl on itself. As you make this scraping movement the top of the paper must be supported against the blade by the thumb of the hand holding the knife (Fig. 21).

You will need to try this a number of times before you are able to do it convincingly. As you practise on strips of paper you should understand that the action of drawing the knife along the undersurface disturbs the tension on one side of the paper, and that this disturbance must be evenly spread on the paper if it is to spring into a pleasing curl.

You will realise, as you practise, that an increase of pressure between the knife and your thumb will result in a tighter curl. But if the pressure is too great you must expect the strip of paper to snap at the point where it is held.

With practice on a number of different strips you should be able to get the feel of the movement and an idea of the amount of pressure required. When you are able to make a satisfactory curl you can gain further experience by applying the technique to actual models. As a first exercise you can change the appearance of the mask (Fig. 20) by curling the points of the moustache instead of scoring and part-folding them.

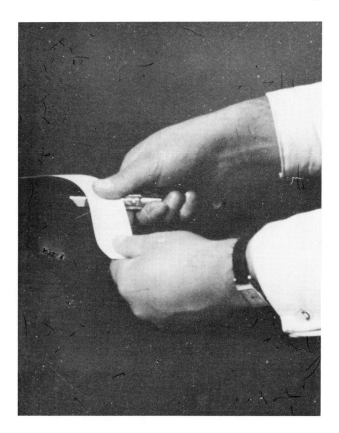

Fig. 21. In the technique of CURLING, the knife should be drawn along the underside of the paper, which must be supported at the top with the thumb. For the paper to spring into a neat curl it is necessary to maintain an even pressure between thumb and blade when using this technique.

The exercise at Fig. 19 can also be given added interest through the use of this technique. But in this case you must make the eye shapes large enough at the top to be cut into points for curling. When you look at the illustration you can decide for yourself whether the whisker shape improves or, in fact, detracts from the finished appearance of this mask (Fig. 22).

Exercises in Combining the Techniques

At this stage in your work you should be ready to attempt combining all the techniques you have learned in one exercise.

Fig. 22. Exercises already attempted can be given further visual interest by using the technique of curling.

Fig. 23a

Fig. 23b

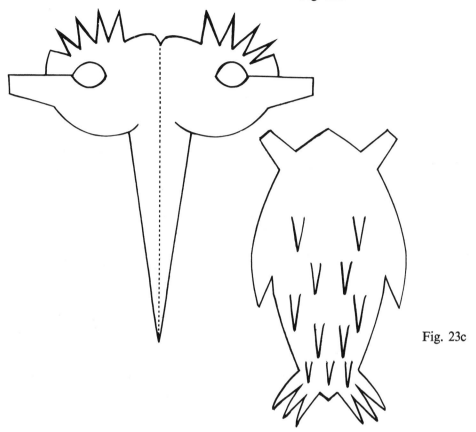

Fig. 23c

Fig. 23. The shapes illustrated can be used as an exercise in combining all the techniques practised so far. The top shape must be scored and cut double, the eyes raised by cutting to the centre, and the shape fixed to the background with the returns. The background must be cut proportionately larger than the eyes, and can be given added interest by raising and curling points on the body.

To make the upper shape shown in the diagram (Fig. 23b) you will find that you must include three techniques: a SCORE down the centre of the shape, a CUT TO CENTRE and a RETURN on each side. If you raise the cones at the circles by overlapping at the cuts the shape can be made up to suggest the eyes and beak of a bird.

The lower shape in the diagram can be cut to make the body of an owl. But in this case a number of V-shaped cuts will allow you to raise and CURL points of paper away from the body shape. You must curl each of these points with some care with the blade of your knife, and they must be made large enough to enable you to hold them at the base as you make the curls.

As a further exercise you can cut into the top edges of the eyes, leaving thin points in the shape which can be curled slightly forward to suggest eyebrows.

The two shapes can be fixed together by cutting slots for the returns in the body shape, and the final model secured to a background by means of the returns included at the top.

If you are able to manage the technique of cutting and curling the points on the body you have reached an important stage in the craft. You are, in fact, able to decorate and suggest further form in your models by cutting into the paper and manipulating it rather than by adding paint. This modelling in the paper itself is closer to the real business of sculpture than models made in paper and decorated by the addition of other materials. It enables you to achieve a cleaner effect in the finished model, and is ultimately more satisfying in that it is work of a type complete in itself.

Painting your models is not wrong; you will often find it necessary to do so in subsequent exercises. But it is desirable in paper sculpture to do as much of the modelling as possible by cutting and shaping rather than by painting.

If you found it possible to employ the basic techniques of paper sculpture in the exercise you have just completed you can now attempt their further combination in examples of really creative work in paper.

You will find later in the book set exercises with detailed instructions in the processes involved in making the models. Attempting these will give you an increased ability to control and manipulate paper, but you should pause occasionally as you go through the exercises to think imaginatively for yourself.

You managed (Fig. 19) to make the head of a cat, which you later improved by introducing the technique of curling. You might now try to evolve a way of making this into a lion instead of a cat. This will require a basic shape large enough to allow you to cut into the sides to make points which can be curled to suggest a mane.

If you can do this you can further improve your ability to model by devising a suitable body shape. This shape can have a scored and curved tail and painted or cut decoration. The return which you included in the cat's head will enable you to fix it to the body.

If you can make one cat you can make a whole row of them with interesting variations of shape and decoration.

Notice that the four cats suggested in the illustration (Fig. 24) appear different, although they could be made using the same technique in each case. If you look closely at the illustration you will see how they are different. You will notice that the head of each cat is suggested in a different position on the body, and that each body is cut slightly different from the next in its original shape. The decoration is also slightly different in each case and you will notice also that the tails can be made to hang down or stand up.

The imaginative development of your work is as simple as this. It is a question of pleasing yourself; doing what you want to with your models and varying them so that they are, as far as possible, interesting and exciting to look at.

The dog in the same illustration could be developed from the same basic shape, and would provide an interesting contrast in a decoration on a wall of a row of cats like the one illustrated.

Fig. 24. When you have practised and understood the four techniques already described you can undertake a project of your own. You can use this illustration as an exercise in the imaginative development of shapes.

You can try something like this for yourself. The illustration will give you the point from which to work. In this case it is a picture which you have before you. If you can make this series of models satisfactorily the next stage is simple. It is merely one of forming your own pictures in your own mind and using these as the point from which to develop your work.

If you are still uncertain of your own imaginative ability you can go back and experiment with other exercises in the book. The bird-shape (Fig. 23) can, for example, be varied by altering the shape of the body and by positioning the eyes and beak at different points on the shape. This is, in fact, a type of drawing with paper which can greatly increase the scope of your work.

Fig. 25. The bird you made in a previous exercise (Fig. 23) can be varied imaginatively by cutting different shapes for the body and positioning the eyes and beak at different points on this shape

If asked to draw a bird many of us will tend, perhaps through habit and lack of imaginative effort, to draw a simple side view of it—usually facing the left. But if we think about birds or—better still—really look at them we can expect to see them adopting a large variety of different shapes and poses as they hop about and settle in the positions which happen to suit them at the moment.

It is this type of variation, imaginatively introduced into paper sculpture, which provides an element of surprise and adds to the attraction of any paper modelling.

You can demonstrate this for yourself by experimenting and playing with shapes. When you add one shape to another—as in the case of the bird—it is not essential to make the fixture at the centre of the shape. If you use the shapes illustrated in the original exercise you will find, by introducing variations in position and arrangement, that you can make any number of birds of different appearance.

This variation in positioning, used freely and imaginatively in subsequent exercises, will give you results which are to a great extent your own work rather than exact copies of the illustrations. And this will add interest to your work as you go on with the exercises.

If you branched out on your own in the previous exercise and found it possible to model the cats successfully you can ignore the exercise illustrated in Fig. 26. This is included for the benefit of those who still doubt their ability to work on their own.

Fig. 26. With a little forethought, it is possible to cut out the cats (Fig. 24) from one sheet of paper. The additional parts of the face can be cut from scraps left over from previous exercises. The arrangement of the two shapes in this exercise may be varied both in the original rectangle and when combined together to make the model.

The diagram shows a possible method of cutting the body and head of a cat from one piece of paper with a minimum of waste. This becomes an important consideration in your work when you reach a sufficiently high standard to be using a good quality paper.

In the diagram the black lines indicating the necessary cuts are marked as close to the edge of the paper as possible. But the returns are included in the planning and placed at points where they do not cause a large waste of paper. This must be considered when cutting shapes with returns.

The tail of the cat can be scored along the curve of its shape so that when it is part-folded it will stand forward from the body. The head can be completed as in previous exercises and fixed to the body in a suitable position.

In this exercise if you vary the placing of the tail in the original flat cut you will find it possible to achieve a variety of different effects in the finished models. Altering the placing of the tail will also allow you to vary the final positioning of the head, which will again change the appearance of the model.

You will find it possible to develop the variety of cats suggested in the previous exercise if you introduce this type of change in the drawing of your original shapes.

To make these changes you are assisted if you cut the models from papers of different size and shape. A long thin shape will, for example, give you a tall cat, and a square shape a much rounder one. If you can learn to exaggerate these peculiarities of shape in your original planning you will find it gives added and amusing interest in your finished work.

THREE-DIMENSIONAL MODELLING

If you are familiar with the term, you may have begun to realise that most of the exercises you have attempted so far have been exercises in RELIEF modelling. You have given form to flat paper and made your models stand out from their backgrounds, but they have in only one instance been completely round.

Your row of cats, for example, can be fixed to a wall and they may be looked at from the front or the sides. But they were not made to be seen from the back. They are, in spite of the fact that they have form, models with only one side. They are pictures with raised surfaces, and as such they are not three-dimensional as sculpture should be.

For you to understand this more fully you should attempt an exercise in real three-dimensional modelling.

In the exercises on raising a cone by cutting to the centre of a circle you were technically involved in three-dimensional modelling. If you made the clown or tiger suggested in this exercise you could have placed it on a table and viewed it from any point round the table. In this case you would have been able to see the front and sides of the model and also the back.

The caterpillar (Fig. 27) is a similar exercise. When you have made it you will be able to see it from these different points of view; and—more important—it should be interesting as a model from any angle.

To make the model you should cut six or eight rectangles of paper (approximately the size of this page) to the shape shown in the diagram. These should all be the same size, and if the papers are held firmly together it should be possible to cut several of them at once.

The centre cut at the bottom of each rectangle will enable you to give form to each of the flat shapes by overlapping the sides; and in each case the overlap should be secured by one of the methods already described.

The two outer flaps at the top of each shape should be pulled together under the pointed pieces. These can be secured on one shape by fixing to the next rectangle as shown in the diagram.

This method of joining a number of shapes together will give an interesting flexibility to the model. You will find this demonstrated as you assemble the caterpillar; it can be twisted and turned along its shape because the joints between the rectangles act as hinges. This method also assists in the development of the size of a model, as in this case in which the caterpillar can be made larger by the addition of more shapes. You can, in fact, cut and assemble as many sections as you like.

For a good visual effect you can, when you understand the method of making up the

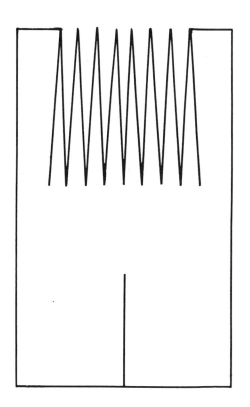
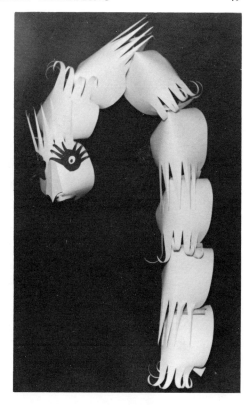

Fig. 27. The caterpillar can be made by joining together a number of rectangles cut as illustrated in the first diagram. After raising form at the front of the rectangle it can be secured to the next by overlapping the two outer flaps under the pointed sections and fixing with a paper fastener to the front of the next rectangle (illustrated by arrow). The head can be made on the first section, using one of the methods described in previous exercises.

model, curl the spikes on the caterpillar's back, or you can score down the centre and part-fold them. An interesting effect can be achieved by alternating between scoring and curling.

To complete the model it is necessary to cut and add a face to the first section. This can be done by one of the methods used in previous exercises.

After assembling the caterpillar you will see that it is three-dimensional and not just a raised picture. It can be pinned to a wall or to a curtain, but it can also be placed on a flat surface like a table and can be seen from all sides.

If you make the caterpillar in bright colours it can be used as a decoration. Its flexibility allows it to be fixed in interesting places. It can be curled over a banister or round the back of a chair—it can even be pinned upside down on a ceiling. In fact, it can be placed in any position since it can be seen from any point of view. And this is because it is three-dimensional.

Exercises in Three-Dimensional Modelling

When you have modelled the caterpillar and have understood what it is to work in three dimensions you are ready to embark on an aspect of the craft in which there is scope for a great deal of experiment.

Paper, unlike most modelling materials, is very light and even the largest models made in paper have little weight when they are completed. With normal types of sculpture it is usually necessary to have a surface on which to stand the finished model. This limits the field in which the sculptor can work, in that his models must be solid and capable of supporting their own weight.

But paper models can be made to hang as well as they can be made to stand. The fact that they are almost weightless offers unlimited opportunity in their decorative use as suspended objects.

In previous exercises most of your models have either been made to stand or you have had to fix them to a suitable background. You can now begin to investigate the use of space.

If you look around you there are probably various decorations on your walls or on any suitable flat surfaces in the room where you are. But if you look up there is probably a lot of empty space under the ceiling. As a paper sculptor you can use this space.

You can make a beginning by developing simple hanging shapes. The simplest of these can be made in thin cardboard, which can be cut to any shape and decorated on both sides. After decorating it, either by painting or by cutting into the surface, the shape can be suspended by cotton from the ceiling. A pin or a small piece of transparent sticky tape will make a harmless fixture.

If you look at the shape after it is hung you will see that it moves slowly; and although it is flat and without form, it occupies in one complete revolution as much space as it would need if it had three-dimensional form. It can be regarded therefore as a piece of sculpture. If it is hanging in a room you can move anywhere in that room and you will be able to see at some time every part of the model. It will, in fact, show the whole of itself as it revolves.

This is a MOBILE, a type of sculpture which moves in space. But the first mobiles you make will be merely decorations.

In Fig. 28 you can see illustrated a suggested progression through a number of simple hanging shapes. The first of these is of the type you have already made. It is one shape only and its movement in space is a simple rotation.

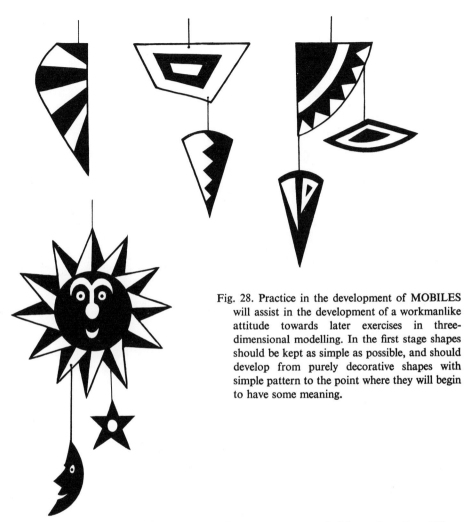

Fig. 28. Practice in the development of MOBILES will assist in the development of a workmanlike attitude towards later exercises in three-dimensional modelling. In the first stage shapes should be kept as simple as possible, and should develop from purely decorative shapes with simple pattern to the point where they will begin to have some meaning.

In the second illustration there are two shapes, one suspended from the other. When you hang this mobile the pattern of movement and the form it makes become more complicated, and the model is slightly more effective as a decoration. This is so because the movement pattern has more variety than that of the single shape.

To make this effectively you must understand the technique of hanging a mobile. When there are two or more shapes in a mobile the lower one must be strung first. Having cut the shapes you must take the lower one and find the point of balance at its top. This can be found by putting a pin through the shape where the point of balance is likely to be, and holding the pin when it is stuck in the cardboard. If the balance is not right you can find the real point at which to insert your cotton by a trial and error process, making new pin holes until you can hang the shape as you want it.

After fixing a cotton to the lower shape it can be tied anywhere on the bottom edge of the upper shape. The point of balance on the top shape can now be found and the composite mobile can be strung and hung in position.

In the third illustration there are three different shapes in one mobile. To make this up it is again necessary to find the point of balance in each of the lower shapes. These can then be fixed anywhere on the main shape before finding its point of balance.

After trying these purely decorative exercises you can attempt something like the final example suggested in the illustration. In this one you can incorporate an element of realism. If you cut and paint your shape to represent a sun, the mobile—besides being decorative—now begins to make a statement. It has a slight meaning, and is in a very simple way a piece of sculpture. It is light-hearted and not very serious, but we have already found that paper sculpture responds well to this sort of approach. The mobile incorporating a sun is not a scientific illustration. It is a gay decoration and it should be treated in this way when you paint it. Any colours you use should be bright and attractive, which is a point to be watched as you progress from these simple mobiles to later exercises in which you will incorporate all the techniques of paper sculpture.

For further exercises in paper sculpture in space you should try to develop an imaginative use of your material as a means of decoration. Paper sculpture decorations are not just paper chains. They are creative works—like the end products of any craft—and they can be far more effective than chains or bought decorations. And since decorations are normally used for gay or festive occasions you should try to make this type of work in paper amusing expressions of your imagination.

Fig. 29a

Fig. 29. An imaginative approach to simple MOBILES will result in the development of unusual and exciting shapes. These should be gay and decorative and, since they must be effective when seen from a distance, should be direct and not over-complicated in detail.

Fig. 29b

The exercises suggested in Fig. 29 are again not very serious. You can make the fish any shape or colour you like. This is a mobile you should attempt because it is developed experimentally in later exercises, but when you attempt it you need not copy the illustration. You can—if you prefer—shut the book and devise shapes of your own for the fish.

The second illustration will remind you of the fact that you have already mastered certain techniques. If you look closely you will see that the two clowns are identical in shape and can be cut by scoring and folding the cardboard double. In this instance the use of two shapes cut from one piece of card might be as effective as the use of two separate shapes in a mobile. There is some point in the shape—one clown holding up the other—and the point is best made by keeping the two shapes together.

In the next illustration (Fig. 30) there are two further suggestions for mobiles. You can try these as exercises or you can develop others from your imagination: a

Fig. 30a

witch on a broomstick, or a balloon with figures in a basket—anything, in fact, which can be reasonably hung can be attempted.

There are many subjects you can choose, but in every case you should aim for a basic simplicity. After you complete and hang a mobile it will be seen from a comparative distance. And involved details, which may take a lot of time and care to complete, will be wasted. If the mobile is moving it will be impossible for anyone to subject it to a very close scrutiny. It must make its impact boldly and almost at a first glance.

This is why hanging shapes made up of several component parts are good exercises in paper sculpture. They provide the sculptor with the need to work boldly and to make direct statements in the simplest possible way. You will find that this applies in all the exercises you attempt, particularly if you compare the results of your work. The most effective pieces of work are likely to be those which make such a direct statement that they can be understood and appreciated immediately when seen from a distance. If your work is fussy and cluttered with unnecessary detail you will find that you have wasted both time and paper. This is bad craftsmanship and is a trap you can avoid by reminding yourself constantly of the need to keep your work as simple as possible.

The introduction of form into mobile shapes can begin in a simple way. The first step in this direction is illustrated in Fig. 31 in which a method of adding to the original

Fig. 30b

Fig. 30. Mobiles are intended to be seen from a comparative distance and should make an impact boldly and almost at a first glance.

Fig. 31. Further form can be given to flat mobile shapes by inserting other shapes through slits cut in the main body. These will give added interest to the mobile as it revolves.

shape is shown. A piece of cardboard or paper cut to shape can be fixed where required by passing part of it through a slit cut in the original shape. The extra material should be scored and cut double—like the fins for the fish—so that it is the same on both sides and will not upset the balance of the mobile.

The fish mobile suggested in Fig. 29 can be developed in this way so that each fish takes on a different appearance as it revolves. In the original exercise the fish seen from the front was only the thickness of the cardboard. With the addition of simple fins it begins to have more form from any point of view, and is consequently closer to being three-dimensional.

The witch suggested in Fig. 31 can also be treated in this way with the addition of a mop of hair, and you now have the technique for curling this hair if you wish.

If the slit in the original shape is cut accurately the additional material should remain in place of its own accord. But if you find it necessary to make a fixture, the smallest piece of transparent sticky tape will hold the shape together.

After making the additions suggested in the previous exercise your mobile shapes will in some cases be almost three-dimensional. You must now consider the problem of giving them real form in themselves so that they can be accepted as examples of sculpture as well as amusing decorations.

There is no way of solving every problem in paper sculpture with a series of cut and dried rules. You must learn rather to tackle the problems as they arise in a workman-like way. There are some simple basic forms—as you will see in later exercises—on which almost any work in paper sculpture can be developed. But before learning to rely on these you should develop a confidence in manipulating and handling paper through all the stages necessary to a model. And you can only be a confident sculptor if you understand in detail the problem in which you are involved as you create any particular work.

If you take one of the fish shapes in the mobile you have made, the basic problem—after you have added fins—is that of giving form to the body of the fish. It should have a top and a bottom as well as the two sides it has in its original cut shape. More explicitly it should have a belly.

A second problem, since the model is to be hung, is that the form needs to be designed so that it is best seen from a point beneath it.

To solve these problems you must begin with a flat piece of paper—since all your problems in the craft must start from this point. If you hold the flat paper above you so that it can be seen from underneath you will find that you can begin to give it form if, holding a side of the paper in each hand, you raise the hands upwards and bring both sides of the paper together.

If you now hold the two sides together lightly between the fingers of one hand—and if you have made the upward bend without buckling or creasing the paper—you will see that it has taken a pleasing curve along the lower part of its shape.

This solves one of your problems. You have a curve suitable for the belly of the fish when seen from underneath. But you must now manipulate parts of the paper to make this curved form suggest a particular shape.

But paper is not like other modelling materials. You cannot pull it or pinch it into shape merely by deciding that a shape should be there. In this case the shape must suggest a fish, and the belly needs a mouth, at its front end. Remembering previous exercises you should be able to cut a separate shape for the mouth and add this to the original paper. This would make your shape more fish-like, but without some cutting of the first piece of paper the result might tend to be rather more crude and ungainly than you want.

Most fish have some elegance of shape. There are oddities and exceptions, but in general terms when we imagine the shape of a fish we think of streamlining and of a form which is complete in itself—rather than of a form made up of a collection of different bits and pieces.

To make this sort of form effectively it is usually necessary to cut and model the original shape. And the cuts used must be designed to produce certain characteristic changes in the form of the paper.

The two exercises which follow should be attempted so that this process of cutting and manipulating may be understood by direct practice in the use of a single piece of paper to give form. In the first exercise the end product is a fish, and in the second a similar piece of paper cut in different ways will produce the form of a bird. These are two different shapes but the method is similar in both cases.

In the exercises you are recommended to follow the processes stage by stage as they are illustrated. Afterwards when you are able to make both the fish and the bird—and when you have understood the processes involved in their modelling—you can try taking a third piece of paper and evolving cuts to produce a shape of your own. If you have really mastered and understood the two exercises a third shape will not be difficult.

To Model The Fish

1. Cut a rectangle of good quality paper approximately quarter Imperial size— 15 inches by 11 inches.

2. Make six cuts in this paper as indicated in the first diagram. You should remember that when following a set exercise it is important to make your cuts correspond in position and length with those in the diagram. In this instance the cuts do not remove any part of the rectangle.

3. Hold the paper in two hands with your thumbs immediately under the cuts at the top.

4. Let the V-shaped section at the top (above your thumbs) drop slightly forward away from your body, and catch the two points at each side between your fingers and thumbs. Finger and thumb on each side should be touching the face side of the paper.

5. Draw the four points together to the middle and fix with a paper fastener. This process allows you to retain the curve in the belly of the shape and at the same time makes a compact opening that will suggest the mouth of the fish.

6. With the model held in one hand pull the bottom edge of the rectangle upwards and forwards to make the top of the body. The two V-shaped cuts in the lower sides of the paper should be left sticking out at the back of the model to suggest a tail. The bottom edge of the rectangle must be fixed in position at the top of the form on both sides.

7. Cut away part of the top of the model where it can be seen to suggest fins.

8. Decorate in the usual way, exaggerating the eyes; thread and hang from the top.

This is not a complicated process, and although it may require several attempts

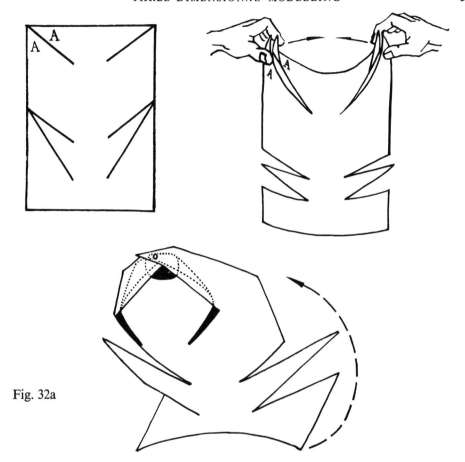

Fig. 32a

Fig. 32. The fish shape can be modelled in three dimensions from a flat rectangle by making the cuts illustrated in the first diagram. The form is raised from the flat by pulling the sides together and fixing at the front (second and third diagrams), and by raising the bottom edge of the rectangle to the top of the model. Further cut and painted decoration can be added as required, but this should be designed to give added effect to the model when it is seen from below. It is not necessary to decorate that part of the model at the top which will not be visible when the model is hanging. Further instructions on next page.

before you can perfect the model, you should be able to raise the paper to a satisfactory form if you understand the reason for the cuts.

The cuts made from the top corners allow you to bring the sides of the rectangle together and still retain the form of the curved belly. They also make it possible for you to ease the top edge of the paper in the form of a cone into the body. This results in a funnel-like shape at the front of the model which is so positioned that, viewed from under the main shape, it suggests an open mouth.

The cuts in the lower sides of the rectangle allow you to raise the bottom of the paper

Fig. 32b

Fig. 32c

to the top of the model without disturbing the curved form which you have already made and which is the basis of the shape. It is because the two cuts on each side are made from the same point that the V-shaped tail remains when the bottom edge is lifted to the top of the form.

For practical reasons you will find that a model like this is best decorated before the form is finally fixed. It is easier to work on a flat surface than on a fragile paper form. For this reason you should experiment and make sure that you can manage the model as illustrated before attempting a final version. It is useful when decorating the model to paint the eyes in first as a guide to further decorations.

Fig. 33a

To Model The Bird

1. Cut another rectangle of paper similar to that used for the fish.

2. Study the diagram (Fig. 33) and make the cuts as shown by the lines in the first illustration. In this model—unlike the fish—some parts of the original rectangle will be removed when you make these cuts.

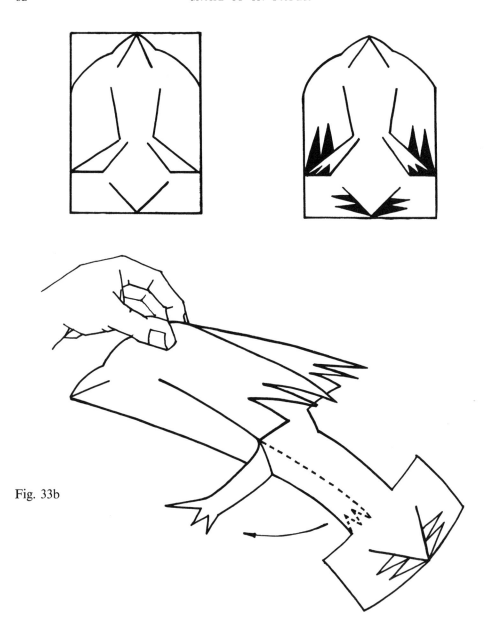

Fig. 33b

Fig. 33. The bird shape can be modelled in three dimensions from a flat rectangle by making the cuts illustrated in the first and second diagrams. After cutting the sides are raised and held at the top, and the legs turned down from the body. To complete the form the bottom edge of the rectangle is raised to the top of the shape and fixed at the point where the sides are held. Added interest can be given by making V-shaped cuts in the body and curling them outwards.

Fig. 33c

3. Cut away further areas of paper as indicated by the filled-in portions in the second illustration.

4. Raise the two sides of the rectangle to meet, and hold them together in one hand.

5. Bend the leg shapes downwards from the body.

6. Raise the two sides of the tail portion and lift the tail upwards and forwards, fixing it into the main body at the point where you are holding the model.

7. Decorate by painting or by cutting into the shape and string with cotton from the fixture at the top of the model.

In this model the pointed pieces of paper at the top of the body may be curled for added effect. It is also possible when modelling the bird to cut V-shapes in the body and curl them after assembly.

In both of these exercises in three-dimensional modelling you started with a flat piece of paper of a particular size, and made cuts in order to assist you in giving it form.

You can now try variations on these forms by altering the size and proportion of the original paper. A rectangle with longer sides will, for example, produce a bird or fish of slightly different appearance from those illustrated.

You can make a further variation by cutting the original shape with the top edge shorter than the bottom. If you employ the system illustrated and adapt the cuts in detail as required you should be able to make a considerable variety of birds or fishes.

BASIC THREE-DIMENSIONAL SHAPES

The fish and bird in the previous exercises were examples of a freely creative type of modelling in which form can be raised by cutting and manipulating one piece of paper.

This is a rewarding method of working with paper, since a sculptor using it must come to the point without a great deal of fuss. And once a particular system of cuts has been evolved for a shape it can be adapted and exploited to solve a variety of problems in paper modelling.

The examples illustrated are, however, only a beginning. There are other systems and methods, some of which you may be able to evolve for yourself.

It is useful in paper sculpture to take a basic shape on which to develop a form. As you go on experimenting from the various exercises it may be helpful for you to consider the use of this system. It can be used in two ways. A model can be complete in itself—made from one piece of paper with variations on a basic shape. Or it can be evolved by taking a basic shape and modelling on to it suitable additions with other cut forms.

These two methods are illustrated in the next exercises. The first in which the use of a basic shape—in this case a cylinder—is shown with a method of developing it to form in one piece of paper. The second illustrates the way in which a basic cone shape can be developed creatively by the addition of various further shapes.

RAISING FORM ON A CYLINDER

A strip of paper, made into a cylinder by overlapping the ends, can be used as a form for the development of a variety of models in three dimensions.

To develop a shape on the cylinder you can begin by working from a plain cylinder and adding separate shapes on one side.

In the fish illustrated the head, tail and fin shapes can be cut and pinned to the cylinder. (These can be cut from odd scraps of waste paper.)

After adding the extra pieces the cylinder can be opened out and the original strip—with extra pieces attached—can be used as a template. This template can now be used on a folded strip of better quality paper. By drawing round the template you will be able to cut the strip with the extra pieces all in one—without any joins.

After cutting the whole shape double and opening it out flat you will find it possible to make up the cylinder again and to fold the added pieces in such a way that they change the basic cylinder to the shape you require. In the case of the fish the two sides of the head can be folded forwards and fixed at the mouth. The sides of the tail can be

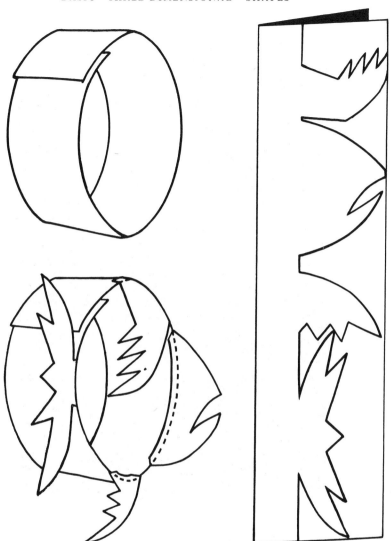

Fig. 34a

Fig. 34. A strip of paper, made into a cylinder by overlapping the ends, can be used as a form for the
development of a variety of models in three dimensions. In this method the whole model is cut from
one piece of paper.

folded backwards and fixed, and the fins can be folded downwards. Eyes and further
decorations can be added as required.

The same system can be used to develop a variety of shapes. To make a bird similar
to the one illustrated you can again begin with a cylinder. On one side of this you can
add a head-shape, a wing and a leg. When this is opened out flat and the whole cut
double the new cylinder can be made up. The sides of the head can be folded forwards

Fig. 34b

and fixed at the beak. The wings and legs can be folded downwards. Cuts can be made into the point of overlap of the cylinder to suggest the tail feathers of the bird.

This method of using a basic shape on which to build a form is one which can be managed quite easily after some practice. It is only necessary to begin with a cylinder and build on to this pieces where they will be required in the final model. This must be done in the first place on the cylinder so that the shapes will be in the correct position when you open the paper out flat.

When the template is made and opened out it can be used to produce any number of the finished shapes—each of which can be raised to form in a few seconds. It is one of the speediest and most effective methods to use where a decoration consisting of a number of models is required.

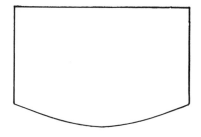

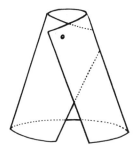

Fig. 35. Three-dimensional forms in paper can be developed on a basic shape. A suitable shape like the CONE can be cut from a rectangle as illustrated, and the shape made up by applying techniques and methods practised in earlier exercises.

RAISING FORM ON A CONE

The second method of raising form on a basic shape is the one in which extra pieces are added to a shape in order to develop the shape into a single model.

One of the simplest and most satisfactory shapes for this purpose, both for hanging and standing models, is the CONE.

A suitable cone can be made by cutting one of the longer sides of a rectangle to a slight curve. This is not essential, since you can make a cone from a rectangle without cutting one of the sides. But it helps when you want the cone to stand upright. Without the curved edge as a base the cone will lean and tend to fall over when you try to make it stand.

After raising the flat paper to a cone shape it must be secured by fixing at the point of overlap—in the same way as your cones were fixed in earlier exercises. But the type of cone you will make from the shape illustrated can be made much larger than those in which you used the Cut to Centre technique. It can be made in almost any size, from paper or from thin cardboard, and after fixing it can be treated imaginatively to serve as the basis for a variety of creative work. The lion in the illustration can be modelled on a basic cone by employing the techniques you have already practised in previous exercises.

If you can make this lion as an exercise from the illustration you need try only a few of the examples suggested. But if you cannot make the lion you should again attempt the exercises stage by stage as they are described.

Fig. 36a

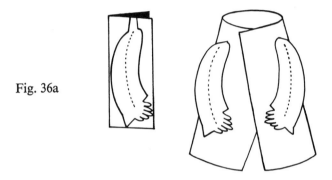

Fig. 36. The diagrams illustrate a possible method of developing the basic shape of a cone into a standing figure by the addition of extra cut pieces.

In the diagrams (Fig. 36) a method of developing the cone into a standing figure by the addition of shapes is illustrated stage by stage:

1. Arms can be cut and scored in order to give them simple form. A return included at the top of the arm will allow it to be inserted into a slot cut at a suitable point in the body of the cone.

2. A face can be made, using the techniques previously employed in making masks, although in this case it must be made on a smaller scale. You should notice that in the diagram the face shape is cut with extra long returns—and that the upper return is even longer than that at the bottom. These returns are necessary in order to establish the head at the top of the cone and to secure it to the body. This can be done by bending the larger return down into the top of the body where it can be secured at the back. The smaller return can be inserted at the front, so that the face is held in position at the top of the cone. Before positioning the face it must be assembled and fixed like a mask.

3. The two returns on the face can be fixed to the body of the cone after insertion at the top. This fixture can be disguised at the front of the cone, where it will show, by the addition of a tie or some other decorative feature. After cutting the tie-shape with

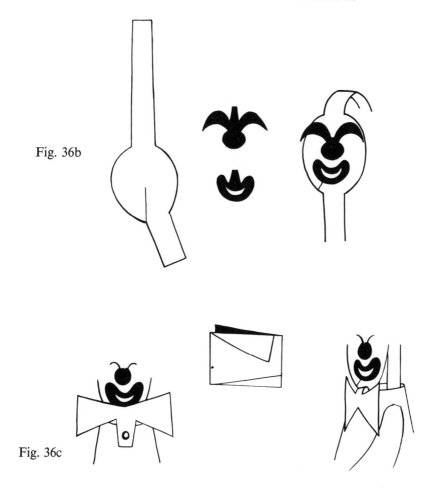

Fig. 36b

Fig. 36c

a return at the top it can be held upside-down at the point where it is to be fixed. A paper fastener inserted through the return will allow the tie to be bent forward to hide the fixture. This is doubly useful since the same fastener can be used to hold the face return in place at the front of the cone.

4. Hair or some other decorative feature can be cut and gummed to the top return of the face where it bends backwards into the cone.

5. Feet can be cut with returns which can be stuck on the inside lower edge of the cone.

6. The model can be decorated in any way to give further visual interest.

If you use the cone or any other shape as a basis on which to build a model you need not limit yourself to figure modelling. There are many other forms which can be built on a basic shape.

Fig. 36d

Fig. 36e

Fig. 37a

Fig. 37. In models based on the cone, the cone can be cut in some cases to assist in the development of the shape. Cutting is best done after the shape is made up, but should be controlled so that as little as possible of the basic shape is removed, otherwise the model will not have the necessary support in the finished version.

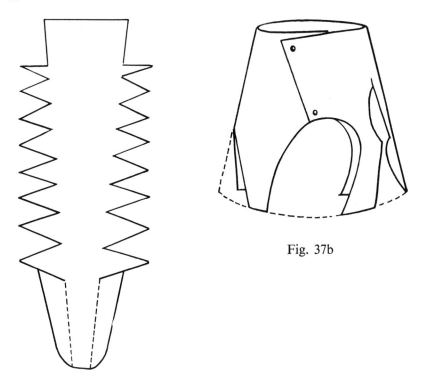

Fig. 37b

The donkey suggested in the exercise (Fig. 37) will demonstrate the wide range of models possible on a basic shape when the shape is treated imaginatively. It will also suggest a further development of the method in which cuts can be made into the actual cone in order to assist the modelling.

Cutting into the basic shape is a useful method of defining shape in a model but it must be done with some care—since every part removed from the cone weakens it as a structure on which to build.

In the example illustrated, parts are cut away at the base of the cone in order to suggest the legs and tail of the donkey. This cutting must be done after the cone has been made up and fixed. If you attempt this exercise and the legs will not support the weight of the rest of the model after cutting, you should remember that the technique of scoring and part-folding along a length of paper will give it added strength. If your model tends to collapse after cutting you can try scoring the legs. If it still collapses after scoring you have cut the legs too thin and must start again.

The head and neck of the donkey can be cut from one rectangle of paper; the lower portions being turned downwards on the dotted score to suggest the shape of the head, and the first triangle on each side being returned upwards to suggest the ears. The remaining triangles can be curled slightly to make the neck more interesting, and the neck itself can be inserted in the top of the cone and fixed where the return is cut.

Before studying further exercises in the use of the cone you should pause to consider its potentialities and its limitations.

The basic cone with added shapes is one of the most simple and effective methods of making animal or human shapes in three dimensions. It can be made in any size or colour, and in most cases it requires little more than a mask and suitable trimmings to complete the shape required.

It has already been said that simplicity and the exaggeration of particular characteristics are among the most important elements in the development of good paper sculpture. And both of these are possible on a shape as simple as the cone.

It is necessary, of course, in any instance of development on a basic shape to have some knowledge of the way paper can be made to behave. This knowledge can be gained by practising and understanding some of the simpler techniques of paper sculpture— like those you have attempted in previous exercises. With a sound knowledge of these techniques and a confident unhurried approach you should find it possible to create almost any shape you want using the cone as a basis on which to build.

But you will find as you develop your work that some models are easier to create than others. There are limitations on what you can expect from paper. If you have difficulty with a particular shape you should consider the nature of the model you are attempting, and try to understand whether the shape you want lends itself to transformation into paper.

A lion has a large and distinctive mane. This is easy to cut in paper and readily identifies your model. A tiger is easy to define because of the distinctive nature of its stripes. But a more subtle shape, like a greyhound or a gazelle, is much more difficult. These are creatures with slender lines and with subtle characteristics which are not easy to reproduce in paper. They are best left to some other modelling material.

When starting any work in paper sculpture you should be convinced that the shape—

in a simplified version—could be possible in paper. If you are doubtful you must experiment and try to make the shape. But a capable craftsman comes to know in time the limitations of his craft.

In paper sculpture these are not many. But they do exist. And if you want to get satisfaction rather than disappointment from your work you must choose carefully before embarking on any creative project.

Your attitude is important. If it is light-hearted and gay and not too serious an attempt to imitate nature your work will have the right sort of touch. And your finished models, being simple and not too ponderous, will be comparatively more effective and satisfying. You will enjoy creating them, and other people will enjoy seeing the results of your skill—as they will appreciate the craftsmanship which you have acquired in order to produce these results.

Exercises in Hanging the Cone

After using the cone shape as a basis for standing models you can investigate its further use in models which can be hung. There are many possibilities in its use as a basis for making good decorations, and the examples suggested in the following exercises should assist you towards the point where you can branch out imaginatively on your own.

If you remember making the owl (Fig. 23) you can use a similar beak and eye shape on the front of a cone. Simple wings can be cut with returns which can be slotted into the sides of the cone, and claws can be cut and fixed at the base. This treatment of the cone should make an acceptable owl which can be further developed with additional cut or painted decoration. If the eyes and beak are large enough they will disguise the cone and make it quite acceptable as the body of the owl. The cone can be used either way up for this model, and when finished is equally effective as a standing or hanging model.

Fig. 38a

Fig. 38b

Fig. 38. The owl (Fig. 23) can be made into a three-dimensional form by cutting the beak-shape
illustrated in that exercise and slotting it into a cone. Further visual effect will result from the
addition of simple wings and claws.

In the next two exercises you can again use the simple cone shape as a basis or you
can introduce a slight development by making your cone from two separate pieces of
paper. This development is not essential and both exercises can be made on a simple
cone. But when the two-piece method as illustrated is employed it provides the advantage
of a contrast in colour between the two shapes, and also gives slightly added strength
to the cone—which might be useful in the development of later models.

To model the angel (Fig. 39) the basic cone can be cut from two rectangles as
illustrated. The larger of these can incorporate the arms; and the two shapes can be
fixed together at the top—where the smaller shape at the front is curved to fit into the
back.

Fig. 39. The basic cone may be cut from two separate pieces of paper, one of which may incorporate the arms. This method gives added strength and allows for effective contrast in colour between the two shapes. To make the angel suitable wing-shapes can be cut and fixed to the back of the cone.

A head can be modelled in exactly the same way as in previous exercises. It can be fixed into the cone by again cutting it with a larger return at the top which can be bent backwards and down into the body of the cone.

A simple shape cut double on a score will give you wings which can be fixed at the back of the cone to make the model into an angel. These are important characteristics and as such they must be given sufficient emphasis in the model. It is really this part which will identify the shape as an angel. Face, hair and other decoration can be applied where you want—and at this stage in your work these should present no difficulty.

The angel you have just made can—if you prefer—be made up as a witch. There are no limits to the variations you can produce once you have understood the use of the basic shape.

In the case of a witch you must make a tall hat to go on the top of the head.

Fig. 40a

Fig. 40. The shape in the previous exercise can be changed by varying the method of decoration.

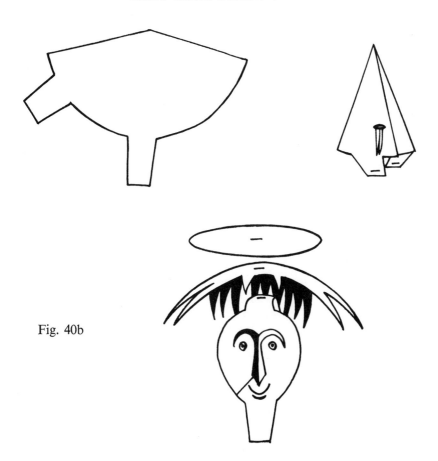

Fig. 40b

A possible method of doing this is illustrated in Fig. 40b. The top shape with the two returns on its lower edge can be made up into a tall cone. This cone will have the returns on opposite sides of its base when it is made up, and these can be used as a means of fixing the cone to a disc of paper or cardboard. This disc will make the brim of the hat. A paper fastener inserted downwards through the two returns on the cone and through the centre of the disc will hold the hat together. The same fastener can then be inserted through a shape cut to suggest hair, and it can be used to fix both the hat and the hair to the top return of the face in one operation. If you use this method of fixing it will help if you pierce all the papers in the correct places before inserting and opening out the fastener. After assembling the hat with the head, the two returns on the head can be inserted and fastened in the top of the cone as in previous exercises.

The tall hat and long hair on the model will be enough to establish it as a witch instead of an angel—although you must, of course, omit the wings which were included in the previous model. But you can add to the effect before hanging by making a suitable broomstick. This can be done by making a tight coil of paper—like a spill—and fixing a curled paper bristle to its end. The coil can be stuck with transparent sticky tape, and the bristle fixed to the coil in the same way. A small hole made in the front and back of the cone body—slightly lower at the back than at the front—will allow you to insert the broomstick right through the model and will give the impression that the witch is riding on the broomstick.

If you cut a third shape (Fig. 41) and add it to your cone by inserting it into the opening at the bottom you can develop your hanging figures still further.

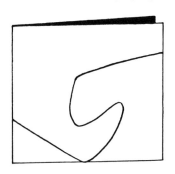

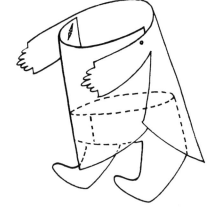

Fig. 41a

Fig. 41. If a third shape is added to the cone many further developments are possible. The shape can be cut as illustrated to suggest legs, and can be inserted into the cone at the bottom. This addition is suitable only for hanging shapes.

With brightly coloured trousers suggested by this shape your angel or witch can now become a clown—although for this you will need to put the right type of face and hat on the model. A suitable hat for a clown can be made in the same way as the one you made for the witch—but this time without the circular brim.

Fig. 41b

To make your models gayer and suitable for decorations you can experiment in hanging them in imaginative ways.

It is easy to fold the arms upwards if you want the clowns to look as though they are holding on to something with their hands. You can, if you wish, fix them to balloons. But for this the cotton must be long enough to tie at the mouth of the balloon and to stretch up and over the top. A small piece of sticky tape will hold the cotton at the top of the balloon so that both the clown and the balloon from which he is hanging can be hung as one decoration.

As a further variation you can make a simple trapeze with cotton tied to a suitably stiff piece of material for a crossbar. You can even hang your clowns by their feet. There are many possibilities. When you can make one clown you can make any number— with as many variations in shape, colour and pattern as you like. If you make them large enough you will find that it does not take many models like this to make an effective decoration in any sort of room.

IDEAS AND PARTIES

If you have studied the various forms of modelling described in this book and if you have practised the exercises you should by now have reached the point where you can branch out on your own. The techniques you have learned will enable you to attempt a variety of imaginative and original work in paper sculpture.

If you have these techniques and a supply of paper you will find it possible to get many hours of satisfaction and pleasure from your work; as you will find that the works you produce, if they are interesting and attractive, will give pleasure to others.

But as well as the techniques and a supply of paper you need ideas and the ability to develop them by using your imagination.

Paper sculpture is a craft which can be undertaken for its own sake. You can sit down and create a shape in paper merely for the satisfaction to be gained from creating that shape. But ideas tend to develop much more imaginatively when the craft is given a purpose.

We have already seen that some of the best results in paper can be achieved when the work is gay and decorative. There are many occasions when decorations are required, and these are the opportunities you should look for to give purpose to your work. But you must understand something of the processes involved in the development of an idea if you are to exploit such an opportunity to its best advantage.

The first step in the process is to choose an idea. For example, if you are intending to give a party and if you want to make it a more interesting party than usual, you can take an idea and work it into a theme on which to run the party.

There are a number of possible themes in the exercises you have already attempted. In several of these you have made fish shapes in paper. With these in mind you might choose an under-sea theme for your party.

When you make this choice the idea can be started in a practical way with the shapes you already know. Your hanging decorations can be those you have already attempted in various exercises. For table decorations you can make mermaids on the cone—as you made the standing figures. Or you can make the mermaids hang as you made the various hanging figures. A simple shape can be evolved and added to the base of the cone to suggest a tail.

Using the cone you can produce a variety of paper hats in fish-like shapes. Or you can develop the idea further by cutting your invitation cards—scored and folded—in the shape of fish. You can use, in fact, every opportunity to exploit the theme imaginatively from the original idea.

Another idea might start with the masks you made in earlier exercises. A number of these produced in animal shapes and modelled in relief can be mounted on top of each

Fig. 42. After learning the techniques of Paper Sculpture and practising their use in the set exercises, you can undertake work on a variety of imaginative projects. Parties and festive occasions are opportunities for experiment in decoration and creative paper work.

other to make a totem-pole decoration. The idea of the masks can now be developed into a Red-Indian theme. In this case your paper hats can be head bands attractively decorated and with paper feathers fixed into them. The feathers can be scored and part-folded to make them stand upright or they can be curled at their tips. For table decorations your cone figures can be made to suggest Indian braves, or they can be simple decorated wigwams. A few bird shapes as hanging decorations will add to the theme.

There are many other ideas and many simple shapes from which an idea can be developed. They are not all included in this book, and if you really sit back and think about it, you will find that you have many more things to choose from in your imagination than you have been shown in the exercises.

Planning a party is always an exciting time. But if you are prepared to work you will find it possible to get even more pleasure—both from the planning and during the time the party takes place—if you experiment and play with paper.

But it is not necessary to wait for a party before you can start work. Paper sculpture can be a hobby. And like all hobbies it can be pursued in any spare moment. You can do it when you feel like it—when, instead of wasting time, you feel the urge to turn to something which is interesting because it is constructive.

In the introduction to this book the craft of paper sculpture was compared to that of pottery. If you wish to develop skill and ability in a craft you must begin by learning some of the techniques. In pottery you could learn these from a craftsman potter. And afterwards, as you practised them, you would find your own skill and ability improving until ultimately you would find yourself able to make very good pots.

By following the exercises in this book you have been able to learn some of the techniques of the craft of paper sculpture. And—through practising them—you have become a paper sculptor yourself.

You may already be a good paper sculptor. Whether this is so or not will depend on you as an individual. Or you may need a lot more practice. You can decide for yourself by assessing your own work. Is it crisp and clean? Is it imaginative? Is it bold and simple and yet still exciting? Or is it fussy and dull—and still rather untidy?

You can only decide by looking intelligently at the work you have done. The answer is in your own creative efforts.

If you have mastered and understood the techniques, and if you are prepared to give a reasonable amount of time and effort to their further practice, you may be sure as you go on with the craft that—no matter what sort of paper sculptor you are now—you will be a better one next year. If you continue to practise and experiment you will eventually, in fact, be a much better one than you are at the point you have reached with the end of this book.

From this point—if you have paper and scissors, and an understanding of the basic techniques of paper sculpture—you can go on creatively in your own way. The rest is up to you.

AN APPENDIX FOR TEACHERS AND STUDENTS

The exercises in this book have been compiled from the work of children and students who have been given the opportunity to experiment in the craft over a period of several years. In order to present them in a way which can be understood by children of various ages they have been simplified and adapted so that a reasonable process of developing skill can be gained from their practice in the order in which they are given.

The type of work which can be expected from a study of the exercises can form the basis of a hobby for an interested child. A child without any previous experience of the craft should be able to develop the necessary interest by attempting the exercises as they are suggested. In the same way the acquisition of skill necessary to progress in the craft may be developed as the child learns and understands the various techniques described.

In planning the process, however, some attention has been given to the potential creative opportunities which may emerge from an introduction of the craft into schools.

In the general pattern of contemporary education the provisions made in schools for creative work in Arts and Crafts are excellent. The majority of children in schools today are given regular opportunity for individual creative expression. This fact must be acknowledged before suggesting that the type of work described in this book might be of interest or practical value to some teachers. It is emphasised that the schemes and exercises suggested are offered only as a supplement to any of the various types of creative work which are already being successfully attempted in schools.

It is to those teachers who might find some interest in the work described that the following points are offered for further consideration:

1. *Creative Paper Work and the Use of Pattern*

Exercise in creative pattern-making in schools is an established aspect of Child Art. It is valuable and popular because children respond well to it. They like pattern making, and most of them have a natural ability to manipulate the colours and shapes from which patterns can be developed. From an early age children gain confidence from exercises in pattern making—as they gain the ability to be freely expressive.

But for children there are certain dangers in a too frequent experience of pattern work. Unless they are treated in a stimulating way and allowed to develop imaginatively the exercises can become repetitive and dull. And as a creative experience practical exercises in painting patterns on rectangles of paper can be in the nature of a soporific rather than a stimulus.

Many teachers, aware of this, have solved the problem by developing their own imaginative approach to the business of pattern-making. In many schools children are introduced at an early age to a variety of media and techniques. They are offered fresh stimuli through the opportunity to experiment and express themselves in new materials. The success of this type of varied approach to the creative work of children is indisputable. It can be seen in the results produced by the children.

It may happen, however, that there are some teachers who are still looking for fresh creative opportunities which can be introduced into their classrooms. Exercises in creative paper work similar to those suggested may be found to be of value in this sort of situation. And a study of this book may provide a useful point of departure for those teachers who are looking for simple ideas and practical methods which they can in turn pass on to children.

2. *The Introduction into Schools of Creative Work in Paper*

The type of work suggested may be found useful when introduced into schools for two main reasons.

In the first place it does not require expensive equipment or special facilities. The work can be attempted in the normal classroom situation. Unlike some crafts it is not out of the question where there is overcrowding or where there is a shortage of money for equipment and materials.

Its introduction may also be of value where Art and Craft lessons are the responsibility of a teacher not specialist trained in the subject. The work in this book is planned for children. But teachers of general subjects might find it useful to extract and develop in their own way those parts which might prove useful supplements to the work they are already attempting.

Many of the exercises suggested can be introduced to children in the form in which they are described. They can be used as a basis for new exercises in pattern-making. A pattern developed, for example, on a fish-shape may be more appealing as an exercise to a child than one painted on a rectangle of paper.

It is only necessary for the teacher to master the exercise himself before introducing it to a class, either in the form in which it is given or in a form adapted to suit the age and ability of the children concerned.

The exercise (Fig. 32) may be used, for example, as a vehicle for pattern work where children seem to be lagging in their response to exercises in shape and colour manipulation. The exercise (Fig. 27) can be used in the same way—although in this case it can be of added value since the individual creative opportunity can become part of communal experience when the results are joined to make the shape suggested.

Opportunities for further experience in pattern can be developed from other exercises (Figs. 8, 9, 10, 15, 17, 18, 23, 24, 28, etc.)

In all of these the value of the exercise as an opportunity for pattern making is increased by the further creative experience the child has in making the model.

The value of this—particularly where the exercise introduces work in three dimensions—cannot be overlooked. The introduction into schools of plastic materials has proved immensely valuable to children. It has provided them with new experiences in their experiments with form. And it has done much to enlarge their understanding and appreciation of the world of art. The convention of the easel painting is no longer the limit of the child's experience of art. Sculpture and modelling are now as familiar to many children as the business of drawing and painting.

The introduction of some of the three-dimensional work suggested in this book may again be a useful supplement to the work already being attempted in this field. Decorative sculpture in paper can be used furthermore to brighten the classroom or studio. And the fact that it can be easily mounted or hung overcomes the difficulty of storage.

Three-dimensional paper sculpture may be of further use in schools on those occasions when festive decorations are required. Christmas is an opportunity for the type of creative project to which children are extremely responsive. Decorations appeal to them. And if they can be allowed to make them for themselves the value of the creative opportunity is obvious.

Teachers interested in the use of paper sculpture decorations will find a number of potentially useful suggestions in this book. But their use in any decorative project can be assisted by the right sort of organisation. Decorative projects may be attempted in two ways:

   (a) A communal decoration can be assembled and hung from a collection of individual experiments in paper. This type of project is valuable to those children taking part, since they will enjoy making the parts of the decoration and will be further rewarded by seeing their own contributions in the finished version of the communal project. But the final result must be expected to be somewhat confused and erratic. As an experience of good decoration a project undertaken in this way might be of less value than one of a more organised type.

   (b) With older children it should be possible—after they have mastered certain techniques in paper sculpture—to encourage individual experiments on a chosen theme. The most successful results can afterwards be selected and broken down to make templates for the production of further similar shapes. The number of these required will be dictated by the size of the space to be decorated. This type of mass-production method is useful in schools where decorations are required to fill large spaces like assembly halls which tend to swallow up thin or timid attempts at decoration. It is, however, a method which requires planning and some control of the total visual effect of the decoration by the teacher. But the final version of the project can be much more satisfying to all concerned than a mixed collection of oddments.

In any work undertaken creatively with paper the main object must be to stimulate and arouse interest in the children. In many cases where children are encouraged to express themselves in a variety of media, additional materials and techniques are unnecessary. The suggestions made in this appendix are offered only to those teachers who are looking for practical and inexpensive aids to the types of creative work they are already sponsoring in their classrooms or studios.

In some cases teachers might, after considering the ideas already suggested, be looking for a simple point of departure for the involvement of whole groups in practical activity. There are times in practical work when it might be desirable or necessary to

Fig. 43. A group of children could work together on a crowd at a football match.

offer every child an opportunity for involvement with a real potential of personal success. It should be possible, for example, on occasions to display the work of every child. If the teacher picks out only the best at the end of an art or craft lesson there will be some children who will never seem to succeed, and some who perhaps, feeling that they are never able to reach the set standards, will concede defeat in the business of practical work at a quite early age. There will be some whose painting will be drab or unimaginative, and some whose work will be tentative or unoriginal and laboured with external influence.

We see a lot of work from children selected for display in schools and in public exhibitions, and this sort of work must obviously go on. But selection and exhibition can tend with some children to encourage a concept of art—a rectangle which if it is good goes on the wall—with standards which they might believe they can never reach.

Tearing or cutting the rectangle in the art lesson where paper is used can occasionally help to topple this sort of fixed concept. If each child can draw the face of someone he knows and, after painting, can cut round the outline, the total number can be assembled together in one group. To stimulate the essential interest factor the group might be arranged visually to suggest a specific place or function. They might be at a football match, wearing large rosettes in their team colours. These can also be cut out after painting and can be pinned to the figures (Fig. 43).

There is a great potential in communal involvement projects when the strict acceptance of the rectangle in art becomes unimportant. For a group at a football match it is only necessary to be able to cut the face and add perhaps a nose. It is not necessary to select the best for display, since the total number can be assembled together into a tight crowd and every child in the class can have work on the wall.

If the teacher can see the potential in this type of involvement activity, and can balance such lessons with the usual type of work in individual expression, he might find it useful to investigate further developments in breaking away from the rectangle.

Where the wall space is wide and not very high, the cut-out crowd could be sitting at a lunch counter with the usual lunch counter objects in front of them. For another exercise every child could be given at the start of the project an imaginary sum of money. This could be varied round the class to stimulate amusement and interest. They might then be sent in imagination to spend the money at a multiple store. When they make their own portraits on this occasion they could include arms and a trunk and could show themselves carrying the imaginary objects they have purchased. The final cut-out results might be crowded together and mounted on a door, as though they were pressed tightly together in a lift at the store. At the side of the door they might include a label with floor numbers and signs indicating up and down.

For girls the portrait group might be at a sale, trying on hats; or a mixed group could be shown examining the exhibits at a flower show, or at market stalls. They could be under cut umbrellas sheltering from the rain. These and other subjects are possible, but in each case the picture could be a composite with every child making a contribution.

If a group is not interested in the idea of assembling a crowd at a football match, or at a boxing match where ropes can be painted right across the display, the cut portraits can be developed in a different context. For a mixed class the subject might be the crowd in church at a wedding—the ladies in new hats, and the men hatless and in their best suits. They can all wear flowers and they can sit in pews which can be painted as part of the exercise (Fig. 44). Another group of children might paint simple stained glass windows which can be set behind the back row of figures at the wedding. There could be an aisle with a patterned floor, arrangements of flowers, and if the children want—a bride and groom. This sort of work can be allowed to grow as far as the children want it to, and as long as the interest is sustained.

Fig. 44. The top figures should be the first on the wall, and the group must be built up from the back to the front.

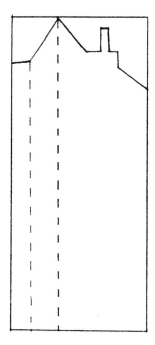

Fig. 45. If the cut-out shapes are folded on verticals like the dotted lines shown, the groups of buildings can be assembled with form in low relief.

The portrait faces may be familiar—people the children know, relations or other children in the group, or their subject matter can be allowed to branch out more adventurously. They could be heads in plumed helmets, and each could have its own shield with a decorative crest. This would involve simple and useful research as a point of departure.

After portrait groups other subjects might be attempted. Houses and buildings could make interesting subject groups. Houses could be drawn as large as the paper and cut out at the outline shape of the roof top (Fig. 45). After painting they could be folded and mounted in low relief, with other visual effects included—lines of laundry, cats on decoratively treated walls, with flowers in gardens and an odd figure group if the children want. After getting used to the idea of communal work children can be allowed to plan and make the contribution they like best.

The scene could be a seaside town with seagulls and boats and with figures on the beach. Or it could be a jungle with large patterned leaves as the individual contribution. These could be cut from paper of varying size and proportion, and could be treated decoratively by the children by direct observation from leaves which they could greatly enlarge on the paper used for the exercise.

When the idea of breaking away from the rectangle and cutting the paper is found acceptable, both teachers and children might find new and exciting opportunities in paper manipulation and exploitation. If this can be developed on a communal basis it might happen that those children who are often quietly neglected in practical work might suddenly find themselves directly and actively involved.

3. *Colouring Paper*

For the type of work suggested in this book a supply of cartridge paper with some thin cardboard is all that is required in the way of materials. For those teachers who would like to develop the decorative side of any work they might attempt to the highest possible standard a method of colouring paper is included in this appendix.

Coloured papers as supplied to schools often suffer from the disadvantage of being well coloured but inadequately flimsy—or of being thick enough in quality but of poor colour. These disadvantages are best overcome where they occur by the preparation of coloured papers by children for their own use.

The colouring process should begin with a supply of good quality cartridge paper. This responds well to dyeing and particularly to the brightly coloured ANILINE dyes which are prepared for theatrical use. These are water soluble and do not require fixing when used on paper.

The dye, available in powder form, must be mixed with hot water in a bucket or large enamel bowl. It should be added to the water gradually and the liquid tested for strength during the mixing by dipping thin strips of the paper to be dyed.

The cartridge paper can be dyed in any size, but anything over full-Imperial size requires special facilities for handling when wet. The paper to be coloured should be laid flat on tables or benches with surfaces protected by several layers of old newspaper. Rope or string lines should be ready close at hand for hanging the dyed paper, and the floor underneath these should also be protected with newspaper.

For applying the dye the largest available brush should be used—the type used for paper-hanging is most satisfactory—and the dye should be applied liberally to the paper with light brush strokes.

After application each sheet of paper should be lifted immediately by the corners and held over the bowl of dye for a few seconds so that as much as possible of the excess dye is returned to the original mixture. If the bowl is large enough the paper can be pulled through the dye instead of being painted. When it is dripping lightly the paper should be hung from the line and left to dry. If aniline dye is used brush marks will disappear and a smooth finish to the paper will be left.

The paper tends to curl slightly as it dries, but this is unimportant and can be eliminated by storing the paper flat when dry.

To avoid unnecessary mess when dyeing a supply of paper it is essential that a good studio or classroom practice should be developed. The process should only be attempted where facilities are adequate or suitable.

If the class is large and space is limited by overcrowding it is advisable to have a working session with the assistance of a few selected children outside the normal lesson time. In suitable weather the dyeing can be undertaken outside the school in a playground or a field. Under any circumstances careful organisation will ensure the best results with a minimum of mess.

A conveyor-belt system works well: one child placing the sheet in position for dyeing, another painting—with a third child passing the dyed paper to one ready to hang it. An extra child hovering with a swab—ready to mop drips from unprotected surfaces—is a useful addition to the team.

The wearing of aprons or other protective clothing is recommended as good studio practice. Rubber gloves may also be worn if available, but these are not essential as the unfixed dye can be scrubbed from hands.

Aniline dyes are available in one-ounce packets from colour merchants. One ounce is sufficient for a large bowl of dye.

Proprietary branded dyes may also be used where the colours are found to be satisfactory. But the theatrical quality of some of the colours available in aniline dye is particularly suitable for its use in decorative work with paper.

4. *Scissors*

The SafeTee Plastic Scissors made by the Platignum Pen Co Ltd, Stevenage, Herts. may be used by children who might cut themselves with ordinary scissors. Their lack of durability is offset by their cheapness.

5. *Conclusion*

The work covered in this book cannot be in any way a complete and final exposition of the creative possibilities of paper. It is intended rather as an introduction to the craft and to some of the techniques which will bring the craft within the reach of children.

There will be times when children attempting the work will meet with failure. When this happens a few sheets of paper will be wasted. But a measure of failures is inevitable in any creative work in which experiment and discovery are essential parts of the process. These failures will be more than balanced by the results of successful experiments, and must be recognised as a necessary part of the learning process.

Creative and experimental work in paper developed from the exercises in this book cannot be attempted in schools where formal drawing and painting are held to be the only bases on which to build the artistic experiences of the child. Any suggestions made are intended to assist those teachers—specialist or otherwise—who believe that the artistic experience of children need not be enclosed within any specified limits. In art all media and materials are of value in the opportunities they provide for expression.

But of all the types of material available, paper is a both cheap and convenient medium in which to experiment. If there are some teachers or students who have considered the suggestions in this book and have been influenced to attempt their introduction to children, it is almost certain that exciting creative developments of the experiments can be safely left to the children concerned.

Those teachers who have learned something from this book have, in fact, learned from the work of children.